SPRINGPI

MORAVIAN MISSION
AND
THE WARD FAMILY
Of The Cherokee Nation

By

Muriel H. Wright

From the Genealogical notes of
Miss Clara A. Ward
And Other Sources

CO-OPERATIVE PUBLISHING CO.

GUTHRIE, OKLAHOMA

To

J. Bartley Milam
In Appreciation

FOREWORD

This story of *Springplace, Moravian Mission,* and its missionaries, is in remembrance of their high ideals, faith, and Christian teachings cherished in the heart of Miss Clara A. Ward.

Clara Alice Ward was born on September 14, 1859, at New Springplace, Cherokee Nation. She was three years old at the time of her father's death; yet so vividly is the scene engraved on her mind that she can still recall the simple funeral services for that brave missionary.

When her mother passed away, Clara made her home with Mr. and Mrs. H. A. Knoll, of West Salem, Illinois. At the age of nine, she was sent to Hope Seminary, a Moravian school in Indiana. Later, she made her home in the East with Reverend and Mrs. W. H. Rice.

Miss Ward completed the nurses' training course at Bellevue Hospital of New York and graduated, R. N., from this noted institution in 1887. She continued as a private nurse for many years and made a high record in her chosen profession. Recently, she has been residing near her relatives in Tulsa, Oklahoma.

It was her privilege to attend the "Old Timers' Celebration" held by the Cherokee Indians on March 3, 1939, at Tulsa. Of this notable gathering, the *Tulsa Daily World* said:

"OLD-TIMERS"

"Men who have come down to us from a former time attracted a great deal of attention in Tulsa recently. Contrasted against a modern setting, these genuine old-timers do much to bring the younger people some rational ideas of those old and totally different days. It is almost impossible for the Oklahomans of to-day to realize the value and color of their background. Much that is meretricious and even trashy is perpetrated in the name of history and legend. But when CHRIS MADSEN for instance, appears, we see the most genuine survival of the days when the principle language of persuasion was that of the gun, and when the protection of a tentative civilization was a matter of men's courage and stamina.

"We are near the time for the fiftieth anniversary of one of the most dramatic of all times—the Opening of Oklahoma. The era represented by the surviving old-timers overlapped territorial days and made vital impressions upon the commonwealth that was to come in 1907. There are not many of these valiant and efficient guardians remaining and we should cherish them and their stories of a brave old time."

Miss Ward felt greatly honored as the last surviving member of the "Missionary Wards" to attend the Old-Timers' Celebration.

Much has been written about the Cherokees for there is a vast amount in original records to prove their story. This memorial volume presents a brief outline of the development of the Cherokee Nation and gives a view of the flowering of Christianity among its people.

Muriel H. Wright

Oklahoma City, Oklahoma
January 24, 1940

CONTENTS

PART I

THE CHEROKEES

PART II

SPRINGPLACE, MORAVIAN MISSION

PART III

THE MISSIONARY WARDS

ILLUSTRATIONS

PART I

THE CHEROKEES

THE MOUNTAIN TRIBE

The name *Cherokee* at once suggests a people whose minds were impressed by the beauty of the spring fed valleys, evergreen mountains, and fertile plains in the ancient tribal domain. Here nature was at its best inspiring vigorous living.

Eastern Tennessee, Northern Alabama and Georgia, and the western portions of the Carolinas included the Cherokee homeland in 1777. A large part of the original tribal domain had been previously given up by treaties with the English colonies, lands which are now portions of the Carolinas, the Virginias, Kentucky, and Tennessee.

At the beginning of the American Revolution, the Cherokees were already resisting encroachments on their lands. The defense of their country was an incentive to the rise of their nation from tribal customs and institutions to those of a modern republic in little more than a century. Its records have every element of epic and the heroic yet involve the subtle points of politics and diplomacy. These make the story of the Cherokees unparalleled in the history of the world, a story in which the deep emotions of a people culminated in the highest expression of the human mind, in art and philosophy.

The Cherokees formerly spoke of themselves as *Ani Yuni - Wiya,* signifying "Principal People." In the records of the De Soto expedition, they were referred to as *Chalaque,* a name from the regional trade language and the Choctaw word *chiluk,* meaning "cave." From this derivation, *Chalaque* would signify "Cave People," or more nearly "Cave Warriors." The Cherokees pronounce this name *Tsalagi* which has been given other interpretations. In some of the oldest tribal ceremonials, they referred to themselves as "People of the Kituwha" (Ani-Kitu'hwagi), the name of an important Cherokee town, apparently the most ancient center from which the tribe spread abroad into a wide region of mountains, river valleys, and southern plains.[1]

In a land of changing colors on the mountain heights, of eerie echoing cries of animals and birds through the dense forests, and of mists rising in the valleys at early dawn, the minds of the people were imbued with belief in the supernatural, in goblins, ghosts, and fairies. Innumerable myths and legends concerning these were told and formed the background of earliest tribal culture, rituals, and ceremonials. While such stories existed as folklore among the people, national myths and legends were only known by the priests or conjurers.

One of these tribal legends related that the people had migrated in ancient times from the West and overcome the original inhabitants of the country where the Cherokees lived in the beginning of the historic period. Another tribal legend and, also, similarities in their languagees indicated that the Cherokees and the ~~Delawares~~ were kindred tribes. Ethnologists have classed them, together with other tribes, as the Iroquoian Family.

The Cherokee language itself was divided into three dialects: The *Elati* or Lower Cherokee, now extinct, was once spoken by that portion of the tribe living in the lowlands, on the Savannah River in South Carolina and Georgia. The *Kituwha* or Middle Cherokee was spoken by the people on

---

[1] Kituwha was near present Bryson City, in Swain County, North Carolina.

* Iroquois
M.H.W.

Cherokee Alphabet.

Sounds represented by vowels.

a as a in *father* or short as a in *rival*
e as e in *hate* or short as e in *met*
i as i in *pique* or short as i in *pit*

o as aw in *law* or short as o in *not*
u as oo in *fool* or short as u in *pull*
v as u in *but*, nasalized.

Consonant Sounds.

g nearly as in English, but approaching to k.—d nearly as in English, but approaching to t.—h, k, l, m, n, q, s, t, w, y, as in English. Syllables beginning with g except ga have sometimes the power of k.—do, du, dv, are sometimes sounded to, tu, tv; and syllables written with tl, except tla, sometimes vary to dl.

Cherokee Baptist Mission Press, H. Upham, Printer and Engraver.

SEQUOYAH'S CHEROKEE ALPHABET.
Old Print from Cherokee Baptist Mission Press, H. Upham, Printer and Engraver.

the Tuckaseigee River in Western North Carolina, to-day the dialect of the Eastern Cherokees. The *Atali,* the Mountain or Upper Cherokee, became the written language. It was the most musical of the three dialects and lacked the sound of *r.*

Earliest accounts of the Cherokees show that both men and women shared in the rights and the responsibilities of their tribal organization. Likewise they both took part in the tribal pastimes of ball plays, games, and dances.

William Bartram, the English botanist, who visited the Cherokees a few years prior to the American Revolution, wrote:

"The Cherokees in their disposition and manners are grave and steady; dignified and circumspect in their deportment; rather slow and reserved in conversation, yet frank, cheerful and humane; tenacious of the liberties and natural rights of man; secret, deliberate and determined in their councils; honest, just and liberal, and always ready to sacrifice every pleasure and gratification, even to their blood and life itself, to defend their territory and maintain their rights."

Though a nation of warriors, usually averaging 4,000 men capable of bearing arms, the Cherokees were agriculturists as well as hunters of big game—buffalo, elk, and deer. Every family had its own small field and every "town" had its large granary for storing corn. Tending the corn crop in all the fields was done by the members of a community working together. In the mornings, during the growing season, the town chief called the people to bring their hoes to the "town house." Thence, they set out for the fields and remained at work until dark, certain ones among the women bringing out the noonday meal. With the men engaged in the defense of the wide frontier of the country in wartime, tending of the corn became of necessity the duty of the women. In the tribal rituals, the spirit of corn was referred to as *Agawe'la,* a beautiful woman.

From a number of estimates made during the century, beginning with 1715, the Cherokees averaged nearly 20,000 in number, living in about 50 towns. Of these towns, Echota (Itsa'ti), also referred to as Chote, on the Little Tennessee River in East Tennessee was the capital during most of this period. Echota was known as the "white" or "peace" town, to which accused persons fled as a place of refuge, to remain until the next "green corn dance," the tribal thanksgiving season in summer, when misdeeds and crimes were judged and generally forgiven.[2]

Gleaming white, the log walled, plastered, and bark roofed houses were built around a central square, in which stood the "town house" where the sacred fire was kept perpetually burning in charge of special guardians or priests. The leading woman of a household made a special request at the "town house" for coals when she needed to relight the fire on her hearth.

Each of the seven principal "towns," really wide communities or neighborhoods, was ruled by a hereditary chief. In the ritual songs of certain dances, frequent mention was made of seven clans which, in earliest times, corresponded to the seven principal towns. The names of the seven Cherokee clans were: *Ani-Waya*, Wolf People; *Ani-Kawi*, Deer People; *Ani-Tsiskwa*, Bird People; *Ani-Wadi*, Paint People; *Ani-Sahini*, Blue People; *Ani-Gatage'wi* (or *Ani-Kitu'hwagi*), Kituwha People; *Ani-Gila'hi*, Long-haired People.

The line of descent in the clan was traced through the mother. The women of each clan selected a leader whose authority was higher than that of the chief when necessary. All the women leaders together made up the Women's Council, at the head of which was the *Ghigau* or "Beloved Woman" of the nation, her voice that of the Great Spirit speaking

---

[2] Echota—Great Echota—was on Little Tennessee River, a short distance below the mouth of Citico Creek, in Monroe County, Tennessee.

through her. So great was her power in the nation that even her wave of her swan wing fan could save a condemned person from death.

At the head of the tribal government in earliest historic times was a great chief or principal chief, referred to in some old English records as "emperor." There was also a great war chief of the whole tribe, who rendered decisions in military affairs and led the warriors in battle. Among other leaders, the next in rank to the principal chief bore a name that meant "The Owl," signifying the same as the title of "prince" in English. The name *Ka'lanu* meaning "The Raven" was a war title, indicating a chief on probation.

The 18th Century was the age of Cherokee heroes under the last of the ancient tribal regime. Old records bear the names of chiefs and leaders who sparred wits in councils with colonial authorities and fought in battles to save the Cherokee country from European colonists to the east, from the Iroquois to the north, and from the Creeks to the south.

The name Attakullaculla (*Ata'gul-kalu*) was that of the civil chief of the Cherokees, long known as the leader in peace councils and early treaties with the English. It was he who saved the life of Captain John Stuart and delivered him safe to his friends in Virginia when the British stronghold, Fort Loudon, in Eastern Tennessee, fell in attack by the warring Cherokees. Continued aggression and arbitrary actions on the part of British colonial authorities caused rivalries and partisan strife within the tribe. Alienated from his former alignment, Attakullaculla raised a force of 500 Cherokee warriors to aid the Americans during the American Revolution, even though a majority of the tribe sided with the British under the leadership of Captain Stuart.

Contemporary with this noted civil chief of the Cherokees, was their great war chief Oconostota (*A'ganu-sta'ta*).

He had the distinction of leading his warriors in a number of fierce battles, coming out victorious without losing a man. It was Oconostota who commanded the Cherokees in their defeat of the Creeks in the battle of Taliwa, Northern Georgia, in 1755. Six years later, he and his warriors stormed Fort Loudon and captured that frontier post. Elected civil chief of the nation soon afterward, he led in terminating the ancient quarrel with the Iroquois. At their invitation in 1768, he headed the Cherokee delegation to Johnson Hall in the Mohawk Valley, New York, where he addressed the Council, "We have come for peace from Chote."

At the end of the American Revolution, the aged Oconostota and his comrades saw their country laid waste and their people impoverished. Yet the name *Cherokee* still commanded respect won by the strength and the character of its leaders in the past three quarters of a century.

THE CHEROKEE NATION, EAST

The new Republic of the United States established peace with the southeastern Indians and took steps to aid them in their advancement as progressive communities. The first treaty between the Government and the Cherokees was made at Hopewell, on the Keowee River, in present South Carolina, November 28, 1785. The United States commissioners advised that the Indians should be paid for lands taken from them unlawfully and that the money thus raised should be used to teach them useful branches of mechanics. Some of the Cherokee women had learned to spin and weave with modern wheels and looms and it was reported, "Many others were very desirous that some method be fallen on to teach them to raise flax, cotton, and wool, as well as to spin and weave it."

In the second treaty with the United States, six years later, the chiefs and warriors were referred to as the representatives of " the Cherokee nation of Indians." For a large land cession (about 2,600,000 acres), the nation was paid $1,000 annually. In addition, farm implements and other tools were supplied by the United States. From this time, the Cherokees rapidly progressed in enlightenment and civilization. With their country well adapted to stock raising, their flocks and herds increased. The sale of their surplus cotton crops brought the comforts and even luxuries of life to their homes.

By 1800, a number of Cherokees had become wealthy planters and traders, owners of substantial residences, Negro slaves, and large herds of cattle. Some prominent Cherokee families were of Irish, German, English, or Scotch descent, their ancestors having settled and married in the nation during the preceding century. They were giving their children the best schooling afforded in that day, through tutors or by sending them to schools in the neighboring states. With the establishment of churches and schools through the unselfish interest of missionary societies, the first of which was that of the Moravian Church, educational advantages in the nation increased.

According to a census of the Cherokees, taken in 1819, there were in the nation "19,500 cattle, 6,100 horses, 19,600 swine, 1,037 sheep, 467 looms, 1,600 spinning wheels, 30 wagons, 500 ploughs, 13 grist mills and 3 saw mills." The next year Return Jonathan Meigs, for many years the U. S. agent and the friend of the Cherokees, wrote the Secretary of War, "that Government aid is no longer necessary or desirable; that *the Cherokees are perfectly competent to take care of themselves,* and that further contributions to their support only have a tendency to encourage idleness and dependence upon the government."

In 1828, the Cherokees were the most advanced of the southeastern Indians. The government of the Cherokee

Nation had been established with a written constitution. In July, 1827, delegates elected from each of eight districts organized in their country had met at New Echota, the capital of the nation, and announced:[3]

"We, the representatives of the people of the Cherokee Nation, in convention assembled, in order to establish justice, insure tranquility, promote our common welfare, and secure to ourselves and our posterity the blessings of liberty; acknowledging with humility and gratitude the goodness of the sovereign Ruler of the Universe, in offering us an opportunity so favorable to the design, and imploring His aid and direction on its accomplishment, do ordain and establish this constitution for the government of the Cherokee Nation."

The document thus drawn provided for legislative, executive, and judicial departments. The legislative branch consisted of a committee and a council, together called the "General Council of the Cherokee Nation." The committee consisted of two members and the council of three members from each of the eight districts, elected every two years. Council sessions were held annually, beginning on the second Monday in October.

The constitution of the Cherokee Nation expressly provided:

"No person who is of negro or mulatto parentage, either by the father or mother side, shall be eligible to hold any office of profit, honor or trust under this Government.

    *   *   *

"All free male citizens, (excepting negroes and descendants of white and Indian men by negro women who may have been set free), who shall have attained to the age of eighteen years, shall be equally entitled to vote at all public elections."

The executive department consisted of a principal chief and an assistant principal chief, elected by the General Council

---

[3] New Echota was on the Oostanaula River, a few miles northeast of Calhoun, Gordon County, Georgia.

every four years. Only native born citizens aged thirty-five years were eligible to these offices.

The judiciary consisted of a supreme court of three judges and such circuit and inferior courts as the General Council should establish from time to time. Judges of the supreme and circuit courts were elected by the joint vote of the General Council. They held their commissions for four years and could be removed from office "on the address of two-thirds of each house of the General Council to the Principal Chief, for that purpose."

It was also expressly provided that ministers of the Gospel should not be diverted from the great and sacred duties of their profession, thus they were not eligible to the office of principal chief nor to election as a member of the General Council.

With adoption of a constitution, Cherokee leaders sought to carry on their plans for establishing institutions of higher learning, a national museum, and the preservation of Cherokee history. Protestant mission schools were largely attended and churches were gaining native converts. The first Indian newspaper, called the "Cherokee Phoenix," was soon published at New Echota, its columns printed in both English and Cherokee, Sequoyah having astonished the world with his invention of the Cherokee alphabet.

SEQUOYAH

Since ancient times, the Cherokee language had been spoken, yet had no written form. Having long contemplated the problem of inventing a "talking leaf" for his people, Sequoyah set to work and within a period of twelve years invented a Cherokee alphabet. Thus, the spark of his genius fired the intelligence of an Indian people: As a nation they wrote their name on the scroll of history. Something of the magnitude of Sequoyah's work is seen when it is recalled that the English alphabet was the result of three thousand years of development by Egyptian, Phoenician, and Greek.

Though he could neither speak nor read English, during the period of about 1809 to 1822, Sequoyah had perfected his alphabet or syllabary of eighty-five characters, representing all the combination consonant and vowel sounds in the Cherokee language.

His curiosity had been first aroused in written words at the time of the defeat of the American forces, under the command of Governor Arthur St. Clair, of Indiana, in 1791. As one of the victorious Indian allies, he realized the importance of the "talking leaves" (letters) found in the pockets of some captive soldiers, though he was unfamiliar with English. He declared to his Cherokee comrades that he could invent a "talking leaf" for the Cherokee people. At the time, his assertion met with derisive laughter and was treated as a joke.

Having visited the Moravian Mission at Springplace and having by chance conversed through his Cherokee friends with a Moravian missionary, his interest had been again aroused in a "talking leaf" for his people. One of the great problems of the German speaking Moravian missionaries in early days was to learn to converse in Cherokee and to be able to translate and publish the scriptures in the native language. Given an English spelling book, Sequoyah studied its pages though he did not know the meaning or sound value of a single English letter. When he had completed his alphabet or syllabary, he had designed thirty-eight characters from his own imagination and made modifications of twelve characters from the English letters. Thirty-five characters had been taken from the old English spelling book, using figures, italic letters, and capitals without regard to their position or value in English.

SEQUOYAH, INVENTOR OF THE CHEROKEE ALPHABET.

Sequoyah was born in the Cherokee country east, in about 1770. As a child, he lived alone with his mother, *Wurteh,* at Taskigi (or Taskeegee), near Fort Loudon, in Eastern Tennessee. She was of a prominent Cherokee family of the Paint Clan, niece of a chief in Echota, and related to the mother of Major George Lowry, of Willstown. Besides his Cherokee name, Sequoyah was known among his people as George Guess, his father having been a white man by the name of Gist (or Guest), who had left the Cherokee country at an early date.[4]

After his marriage, Sequoyah moved to Wills Valley (Eastern Alabama) where he cultivated a small farm and conducted a trading post in connection with a blacksmith shop. He was known for his artistry in charcoal drawings and also became skilled as a silversmith. Once he asked Charles Hicks who was visiting him to write his English name. Hicks wrote it *"George Guess."* Sequoyah made a metal die of the name and stamped it on all his silverwork from this time.

---

[4] Most authoritative writers and students of Sequoyah's life maintain that his father was Nathaniel Gist, a lieutenant in George Washington's regiment at the time of Braddock's defeat in 1755, and later an officer in the American army during the Revolution. Nathaniel Gist when a young man was a trader for a time among the Cherokees and afterward served on a number of Government commissions to the tribe. The statement that Sequoyah's father was a German trader by the name of Gist has not been generally accepted and may have arisen from the fact the family of William Gist, an uncle of Nathaniel Gist, lived near Salem in the Moravian colony of Wachovia, North Carolina, thence moved to Tennessee. Samuel Cole Williams, in his article, *The Father of Sequoyah: Nathaniel Gist* (Chronicles of Oklahoma, Vol. XV, No. 1) quoted the following from the manuscript, *Life of George Gist,* dictated to John Howard Payne in 1835, by relatives of Sequoyah, including Major George Lowry: "The family of Gist, on the Indian side (the mother's) was of high rank in the nation. The famous John Watts was one of them. Two of his uncles were men of great distinction: One of the two was named Tahlonteeskee (the overthrower) and the other Kahn-yah-tah-hee (the first to kill). Kahn-yah-tah-hee was the principal chief of old Echota (Chota as known to the English), the ancient town of refuge over which he presided. He was called the Beloved Chief of all the people. It was his exclusive duty and delight to be a peace-preserver."

Often his preoccupied air during his twelve years of study made people think him demented. Finally, judging him a sorcerer, a band of Cherokee warriors visited him with the intention of putting him to death in accordance with tribal law. Through the influence of his cousin, Chief George Lowry, of Willstown, he was given a trial during which he demonstrated the value of his invention. Before a week had passed, the warriors themselves had mastered the new writing under Sequoyah's instruction. Returning to their homes, word of the Cherokee "talking leaf" spread through the countryside. Within an incredibly short time, usually after a few days' study, a Cherokee could communicate in writing by means of the great invention.

A year or two after perfecting his alphabet, Sequoyah visited the Western Cherokees who had been living in Arkansas for nearly thirty years and taught them his invention. Soon there began regular communication between the Westtern and the Eastern Cherokees, in letters. Old bonds of kinship and old friendships were renewed and a people that had been separating into bands and moving to far away regions were again affiliated in their interests.

Sequoyah made his home among the Western Cherokees and became an influential leader and member of their council. As one of their delegates in Washington, in 1828, he signed his name, using the letters of his alphabet, to the treaty of that year providing for the settlement of all the Cherokees in what is now Northeastern Oklahoma. The next year, he moved with the Western Cherokees from Arkansas to their new country, choosing a location about ten miles northeast of the present town of Sallisaw, in Sequoyah County. Here his old log cabin has been preserved as an historic shrine in Oklahoma.

In 1843, Sequoyah set out on a journey to the Southwest in search of some bands of Cherokees reported living in

CAPITOL OF THE CHEROKEE NATION,
at Tahlequah.

Mexico. In the summer of the next year, he died and was buried at San Fernando, far from his own country. With him was interred his prized silver medal which had been especially made and presented him by the Cherokees in token of their esteem for his wonderful invention.

The American Board of Foreign Missions, at Boston, had furnished a special font of type in the Cherokee alphabet and a printing press had been set up in the nation. The scriptures, tracts, and other religious works, besides textbooks and the Cherokee constitution and laws were printed in the native language.

The noted Sam Houston had once remarked to Sequoyah: "Your invention of this alphabet is worth more to your people than two bags of gold in the hands of every Cherokee."

When the Cherokee Nation was established in the West in 1839, the dissemination of knowledge among its people through the printed word, made possible by Sequoyah's invention, was an inspiration throughout the Indian Territory. It led the way in enlightenment and culture which became the foundation stone of the future State of Oklahoma. The printing press at Park Hill, under the auspices of the American Board, beginning with 1836, published millions of pages in religious works, almanacs, textbooks, and laws in Cherokee and in the languages of other Indian nations and tribes. The Baptist Mission Press at "Baptist," near present Westville in Adair County, did a similar work and published the "Cherokee Messenger," a religious paper, in 1844, the first periodical printed within the present boundaries of Oklahoma. In the same year, the "Cherokee Advocate," published at Tahlequah under the direction of the Cherokee government, was the first newspaper in the Territory.

THE TRAIL OF TEARS

Plans for the removal of all the Indians in the East to a region in the West where they might have their own governments had been promoted by U. S. Government officials before 1820. The discovery of gold in the Cherokee Nation, in 1828, within the boundaries claimed by the State of Georgia, brought a rush of people from the States into the gold region. In May, 1830, an act of Congress provided for the removal of the eastern Indians to the West beyond the Mississippi River. Taking advantage of the situation, many persons from the States unlawfully crowded into the Cherokee country, forcing even wealthy and influential citizens from their homes. The State of Georgia was opposed to the continuance of the Cherokee government within the state's borders. As a result, the Indian question and the removal plan were widely and bitterly discussed throughout the country. The words of Senator Frelinghuysen of New Jersey, the Indians' friend, in his speech before the U. S. Senate, were in the nature of a prophecy:

"I had rather receive the blessing of one poor Cherokee, as he casts his last look back upon his country, for having, though in vain, attempted to prevent his banishment than to sleep beneath the marble of all the Caesars."

One phase of the case of the Cherokees was even taken to the U. S. Supreme Court, of which John Marshall was Chief Justice, and decided in their favor. When the President of the United States, Andrew Jackson, long a promoter of Indian removal, heard the decision of the Court, he was reported to have said: "John Marshall has made his decision, now let him enforce it."[5]

In 1835, a treaty was negotiated at New Echota by United States Commissioners, providing for the removal of the Chero-

---

[5] Thomas Valentine Parker in "The Cherokee Indians," page 30.

kees to the West and the sale of all their domain in the East, approximately 8,000,000 acres, for little more than fifty cents an acre. Chief John Ross's proposal at Washington that the Cherokee Nation be paid approximately $2.50 per acre had been dismissed by Government officials as exorbitant, even though some forty acre plots in the gold region soon sold for $30,000. In view of the desperate situation of their nation, Major Ridge, his son, John, and his two nephews, Elias Boudinot and Stand Watie, were among the leading signers of the New Echota Treaty in a council attended by very few members of the tribe. Chief Ross, Major Lowry, and other prominent leaders, representing a large majority of the people, mostly fullbloods, were bitterly opposed to the terms of the treaty.

Not long after the negotiations at New Echota, members of the Ridge Party joined the Western Cherokees or "Old Settlers" in the Indian Territory. The latter had moved to this region from Arkansas by the terms of the Treaty of 1828, which had provided 7,000,000 acres in present Northeastern Oklahoma and the "Cherokee Outlet" (a tract of 6,000,000 acres to the west) to be owned and settled by all the Cherokees.

About 16,000 members of the Ross Party, nearly two-thirds of the nation, refused to leave their country in Georgia, remaining peaceably in their homes. It was said the Cherokee women were the leaders in this. Chief Ross's efforts to have the treaty annulled at Washington were of no avail. Matters cames to a crisis in the summer of 1838. General Winfield Scott, carrying out the orders of President Jackson, established military headquarters at New Echota and issued a proclamation that every Cherokee man, woman, and child must be on the way west within thirty days. The people still waited hoping that Ross could secure some modifications of the Treaty. The end came with General Scott's orders. Soldiers with rifles and bayonets drove the startled Cherokees from their homes, many times with oaths and blows, to stockade camps. Suffering the bitterest deprivations and hardships, the emigrants were conducted thence in large groups, on horseback, in wagons, and thousands on foot, under military supervision.[6] In the midst of winter storms, the long road west became the *Trail of Tears*. Nearly four thousand Cherokees died and were buried along the way. Many years afterward, an officer in the Confederate Army, who had served as a volunteer in the Georgia troops in 1838, said: "I fought through the civil war and have seen men shot to pieces and slaughtered by thousands, but the Cherokee removal was the cruelest work I ever knew."

THE CHEROKEE NATION, WEST

Chief Ross and his followers arrived in the West in the spring of 1839. The question soon arose who should be the leaders and which of the two groups—eastern or western—should control the Cherokee government. The Western Cherokees maintained that the newcomers should join them and recognize their laws and officers, at least until the regular elections in the fall. Party feeling ran high among the full-bloods of the Ross Party against members of the Ridge Party who had sided with the Old Settlers.

In 1829, Major Ridge had sponsored a law in the Cherokee Council, making it a penalty of death to sell any of the tribal domain. Presumably for having signed the New Echota Treaty and thus failing to obey this law, Major Ridge, John Ridge, and Elias Boudinot were assassinated in different parts of the country at almost the same hour. These crimes were committed by a secret revengeful group unknown to any of the tribal leaders. A feud among some of the people began,

---

[6] "Myths of the Cherokee" (Historical Sketch in) by James Mooney. 19th Annual Report, Bureau of Ethnology.

which together with controversies over the terms of the New Echota Treaty formed the background of political life in the Cherokee Nation for many years.

Despite threats against their lives, John Ross and his friends proceeded to organize the government. In July, an Act of Union was signed in a convention of the two parties, over which Sequoyah presided. On September 6, 1839, a new constitution was adopted in a national convention at Tahlequah signed by *George Lowry,* as president of the convention.

The new constitution was similar to that which had been adopted in the Cherokee Nation East. Elected members of a national committee (senate) and a council (house) together composed the National Council of the Cherokee Nation. The executive branch consisted of a principal chief and an assistant principal chief, with an executive council of five (or three) members appointed by the National Council. Supreme, circuit, and lesser courts made up the judiciary. By 1841, the nation had been divided into eight districts (later increased to nine) and Tahlequah had been designated the capital.

Within five years, the Cherokees were progressing in their new country. Houses and farms were being improved and neighborhood public schools increasing, with a native Cherokee elected superintendent of public schools. Christian churches were gaining converts and a national temperance society boasted 1,762 members. Well selected libraries were found in a number of homes. Thousands of Cherokees could speak and write English and many were able to draw up contracts and deeds, and were shrewd and intelligent in carrying on ordinary business transactions.

Two national seminaries opened in 1851, were notable in the advancement of the Nation. Mr. Oswald Langdon Woodford, of Yale, was the principal of the young men's seminary near Tahlequah. Miss Ellen Whitmore, of Mount Holyoke, was principal of the seminary for young women, near Park Hill. Commencement exercises at the latter were festive occasions—the graduates dressed in white, there was a profusion of flowers and programs of music, essays, and original poems, with prominent citizens, government officials, and principal chiefs attending. The young women students published a magazine called "Cherokee Rose Buds," bearing the motto, *"Devoted to the Good, the Beautiful, and the True."*

Masonic lodges were established in the nation. Through the influence of Baptist missionaries, a secret society was organized among the fullblood Cherokees, called the "Kee-too-wah," (from the ancient name *Kituwha*), to preserve Cherokee history and promote high ideals of individualism.

Aligned with the Confederacy during the war between the states, the Cherokee Nation was a scene of desolation at the close of the great conflict. Nevertheless, by the terms of a new treaty with the Federal Government in 1866, the Cherokees, "numbering fourteen thousand impoverished, heart broken, and revengeful people," began to build again, bending to their "task with a determination and perseverance that could not fail to be the parent of success."

In 1884, Charles Royce, in his history of the Cherokees, wrote:

"To-day their country is more prosperous than ever. They number twenty-two thousand, a greater population than they have had at any previous period, except perhaps just prior to the date of the treaty of 1835. . . .

"To-day they have twenty-three hundred scholars attending seventy-five schools established and supported by themselves at an annual expense to the nation of nearly $100,000. To-day thirteen thousand of their people can read and eighteen thousand can speak the English language. To-day five thousand brick, frame, and log houses are occupied by them, and they have sixty-four churches with a membership of several thousand.

CHEROKEE NATIONAL MALE SEMINARY, 1851.
Southwest of Tahlequah.

"They cultivate a hundred thousand acres of land and have an additional one hundred and fifty thousand fenced. They raise annually 100,000 bushels of wheat, 800,000 of corn, 100,000 of oats and barley, 27,500 of vegetables, 1,000,000 pounds of cotton, 500,000 pounds of butter, 12,000 tons of hay, and saw a million feet of lumber. They own 20,000 horses, 15,000 mules, 200,000 cattle, 100,000 swine, and 12,000 sheep."

A "Cherokee Fair" at Fort Gibson led to the organization of the Indian International Fair at Muskogee, first opened in 1874, for many years advertising the agricultural and industrial growth of the whole Indian Territory. The "Cherokee Advocate" was printed again at Tahlequah, the two national seminaries were re-opened, and the Cherokee Orphan Asylum established.

When the "Oklahoma Country," in the central part of the Indian Territory, was opened to white settlement in 1889, Elias C. Boudinot, son of the late Elias Boudinot, had been one of its prime advocates. When Oklahoma became a State in 1907, a United States senator, a congressman, and many State and county officers had been former citizens of the Cherokee Nation.

It was an honor to the record of the Cherokee Nation that the Third State Legislature of Oklahoma made provisions for the erection of a statue of Sequoyah, in the National Capitol at Washington, D. C.

Less than three decades later, another memorial statue was erected in the National Capitol, that of Will Rogers, world famous humorist and philosopher, of Cherokee descent, and a native of Oklahoma.

THE ROSE OF CHEROKEE

Though beauty deck the spring with flowers
 Like rainbows sleeping on the green,
Or soft through moonlight's dewy showers
 May star-like glitter o'er the scene;
Though passions young and warm may spring
 With rapture through the thrilling heart;
Though earth and sea their treasures bring
 Combined with all that's prized in art—
  Still, wanton Nature's dark-eyed child
   Is far more dear to me—
  The sweetest flower that gems the wild
   Is the Rose of Cherokee.

Though far away, 'neath orient skies,
 Where clouds come not nor sweeps the storm,
The maid may blush in roseate dyes
 Like hues upon an angel's form;
Though every blaze of jewelled fire
 That wealth may shower o'er neck and arm:
Though soft, voluptuous, gay attire
 May heighten every dazzling charm—
  Still, wanton Nature's dark-eyed child
   Is far more dear to me—
  The sweetest flower that gems the wild
   Is the Rose of Cherokee.

LYDIA ANN WARD

Though gorgeous flower flame o'er their bed,
   Adorned by art's surpassing taste,
Their fragrance and their blush-light shed
   When by the lips of Rose are placed;
Though wild flowers spangling every green
   Woo all the stars from heaven's blue deep,
Till eyes of love melt o'er the scene
   And tears of bliss in silence weep—
     Still, wanton Nature's dark-eyed child
      Is far more dear to me—
    The sweetest flower that gems the wild
     Is the Rose of Cherokee.

She is a gay and artless sprite,
   Her eyes are glad and happiness
Plays round her lips in rosy light,
   Bright with the conscious power to bless.
Her heart is pure, as wild, as free
   As yonder streamlet leaping bright;
Her soul's a gem of purity
   And warm as loveliest star of night—
     Yes, wanton Nature's dark-eyed child
      The jewel is for me—
    The sweetest flower that gems the wild
     Is the Rose of Cherokee.

                    —Anonymous**

** The writer was said to have been a student at the Cherokee National Male Seminary. This poem, *The Rose of Cherokee,* appeared in "The Sequoyah," Vol. I, Number 1, published by the students of the Male Seminary, August 1, 1855.

Part II
S P R I N G P L A C E,
M O R A V I A N   M I S S I O N

EARLY MORAVIAN HISTORY

For three hundred years after the defeat of the Bohemian Protestants at the Battle of White Mountain, November 8, 1620, during the Thirty Years' War, Moravia, an old slavonic state adjoining Bohemia, was a crown land of Austria. When Czecho-Slovakia was organized at the end of the World War, Moravia was a part of this Eastern European republic.

The word "Moravian" goes back to the 6th Century when the Russian Slavs came down over the Carpathian Mountains and settled in the valley of the Morava (present March) River, from which the immigrants later took their name. In the 9th Century, the boundaries of the Kingdom of Great Moravia, extending from Western Bohemia to the mountains, were nearly the same as those of the Republic of Czecho-Slovakia, the recent tragedy of which quickens interest in the story of its peoples and the ancient Christian Church. To know that Moravian Brethren had a deep influence in promoting Christian civilization among the Cherokee Indians doubles our interest in this story.

Shortly after the time of Charlemagne, the Moravian people were converted to Christianity by the Greek Monks Cyril and Methodius (863 A. D.). Six hundred years later, the Christian Moravians were followers of the religious leader John Huss, after whose death their organization was recognized as the national Church of Bohemia (1453).

With the passing of years, this Christian organization was joined by many Germans and even spread into Poland. When their allies were defeated at White Mountain, groups of Moravians were forced to flee to other countries,—Saxony, England, and even to far-away Texas.   In Moravia, the communicants who remained continued to worship in secret, their group referred to for over a century as the "Hidden Seed" by members of the Church elsewhere.

When religious persecution broke out afresh in Bohemia and Moravia, the "Hidden Seed" of the Ancient Brethren, most of whom were Germans, were led by Christian David to Saxony.   They established a colony, called Herrnhüt, on the estate of Count Zinzendorf in 1722, and were soon afterward joined by some Schwenfelder, followers of the Silesian nobleman and religious leader, Caspar Schwenfeld.   At Herrnhüt occurred the great revival and "outpouring of the Holy Spirit" on August 13, 1727, which became the birthday of the modern Moravian Church.

Missionary zeal and the carrying of the word of God to every part of the world where the way was open was the spirit of the Renewed Moravian Church.   It declared that true faith was "to know God, to love Him, and to do His commandments."   Church discipline was strict, with members divided into three classes—the Perfect, the Proficient, the Beginners—, and a constitutional government nearly like that of the Presbyterians.   Right living was stressed and conduct rather than doctrine, gained by education especially through the work of the press in books and the printed Word.   A quiet spiritual life was fostered.   Members' families lived in settlements centering in the church and the school, on the estates of friendly noblemen.   In the history of Protestantism, the spirit of the Moravian Church was very important: Moravians were the first Protestants to declare the evangelization of the heathen the duty of the Church.

Beginning with 1732, the first Moravian missions were established in Greenland and in the West Indies.   When an edict of banishment was issued against all Schwenfelder in Saxony, those at Herrnhüt, joined by other Protestant groups from Holland and England, sailed for Pennsylvania, arriving in 1734. Bethlehem and Nazareth were among the names of their early settlements.

Count Zinzendorf secured a grant of five hundred acres for another colony, in Georgia, through the aid of General Oglethorpe, a warm friend of the Church. After a season of prayer and reference to the lot, according to Moravian custom, ten of the Brethren set sail and arrived at Savannah on April 8, 1735, where they were well received by the people of the town.

A second band of Moravians and their families came early the next year to Savannah, led by Bishop David Nitschman, whose face appeared "as the face of an angel" to the earlier colonists. With him was Martin Mack, afterward missionary to the northern Indian tribes. There were also John and Charles Wesley and Benjamin Ingham, of the Church of England and the "Methodist Society." Warm friendship for the members of all Christian churches marked the spirit of the Moravians. Never a large group in themselves, they were noted for their Christian influence and their ministry to the scattered members of other churches without drawing them into their own Moravian organization.

Ingham, of the "Methodist Society," and Peter Rose and his wife, Moravians, soon began missionary labor among the Lower Creeks. The mission was called *Irene* and was located on an island a mile from Savannah. Outbreak of the war between England and Spain, fought on the southern frontier in America, soon brought the work of the school for Creek boys and girls, to a close. Willing to pay double taxes but objecting to taking up arms in the war, the Moravians left Georgia for Pennsylvania, in April, 1740, sailing on the sloop "Savannah."

John Hagen, a lone Moravian, remained in Georgia working among the wounded and dying Indians brought into
Savannah from the fighting on the frontier. In 1742, he also
sailed for the North.

The Moravian Brethren and Ingham had been eager to
begin missions among the Cherokees. Their tribal settlements
far to the west in a mountainous country, reached by narrow
trails, had made this impossible in view of the threatening
frontier war.

Christian Priber, a German Jesuit, working in the interests of the French, had begun the first Christian work among
the Cherokees in 1736. Priber learned their language, adopted their ways, and lived with the Cherokees nine years. A
man of culture and great learning, his plan was to organize
all the Southern Indian tribes into a confederacy opposed to
the English interests. His capture and imprisonment by the
English while he was on a journey among the Creeks and
his death soon afterward, brought this first missionary work
among the Cherokees to a close.

The Moravian Brethren never abandoned hope that the
way might be opened for them to return for missionary work
among the Indian people of the South, especially the Cherokees. In 1745, "The Society for the Furtherance of the Gospel"
was reorganized at Bethlehem, Pennsylvania, into "The Society of the United Brethren for Propagating the Gospel
Among the Heathen." Mission stations were successfully
established among the Delawares and the Mohicans in the
North.

The system of establishing Moravian colonies in America,
closely associated with the Church at Herrnhüt, from which
consecrated brethren and sisters might be chosen as volunteers
for service in outlying communities was adopted as that of
the Moravian Church in America. Having been recognized

by Parliament as "an ancient Protestant Episcopal Church" in England, the Brethren had gained recognition of their liberty for "worship and service" throughout the British possessions.

Among their English friends was Lord Granville, Speaker of the House of Commons, with whom Count Zinzendorf negotiated the purchase of 100,000 acres of Granville's grant of lands in North Carolina. To this large tract in the wilderness, twelve of the Brethren journeyed from Bethlehem, in the autumn of 1753. Their colony was called *Wachovia*, so named because the beautiful meadow lands in this region reminded them of the valley of the Wach on the Zinzendorf estate in Austria. The settlements of Bethabara, Bethania, and Salem were begun, the latter designated as the principal town and the seat of government of the Moravian Church in the South.

During the dangerous times of the French and Indian wars, hundreds of Indians passing on their way through the colony were kindly received and Bethabara was noted among them as the "Dutch Fort, where there are good people and much bread." Many homeless refugees from the frontier American settlements were cared for at Wachovia. Once among them was a poor, sick stranger named Edward Buttler, who many years later was captain of the U. S. garrison at Tellico Blockhouse and Indian agent to the Cherokees.[7]

From time to time, chance meetings with Cherokee chiefs and information as to the character and customs of their tribe kept up the Moravians' hope for a Cherokee mission. In 1765, a letter came to Wachovia expressing interest in the

---

[7] For much of the data on early Moravian missions in America used in compiling this volume, acknowledgment is due *History of the Moravian Missions Among Southern Indian Tribes* by Rev. Edmund Schwarze, published at Bethlehem, Pa., 1923. Records of the Moravian missions among the Cherokees East were kept in German. After the removal to the Indian Territory, mission records were in English.

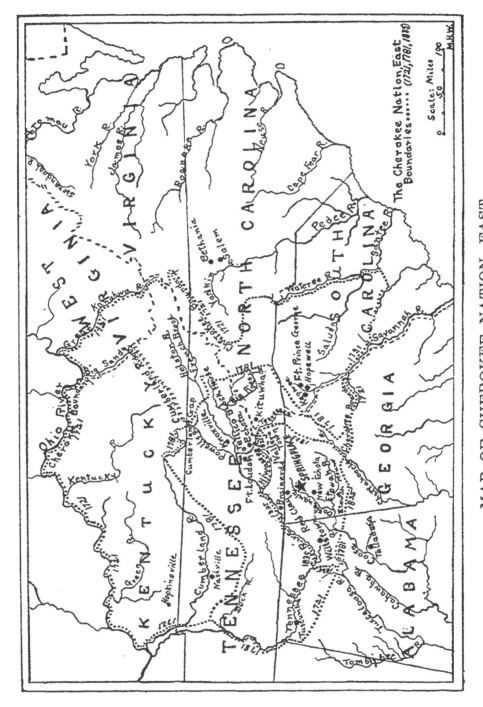

MAP OF CHEROKEE NATION, EAST.

Dotted lines indicate Cherokee boundary lines at end of three periods,—
1721, 1781, 1835.

plan, from John Daniel Hammerer, a Lutheran and religious exile from Alsace, who was located at Fort Prince George (in the Cherokee country, South Carolina) as a Christian teacher. Hammerer had been encouraged in this undertaking by the Governor of Virginia with a fund of $200.00 and a recommendation to Chief Attakullaculla who promised the young man his protection.

In 1773, a Cherokee man and his wife, who were given the names of Noah and Wilhelmina, were the first converts among his people in the Moravian Church at the Delaware Mission in Ohio. The plan for Noah to accompany one of the Brethren to the Cherokee country near Wachovia was interrupted by the outbreak of the American Revolution. Ten years later, Brother Martin Schneider set out from Salem on a journey to the Upper Cherokees on the Tennessee. He was the first Moravian to meet the chiefs at Echota. Disputes over land cessions and threatening war with the Cherokees in some of the states, delayed the purpose of Schneider's visit.

In 1799, conditions had been tranquilized. There was renewed interest in establishing missions among the Southern Indians. Dartmouth College planned opening a mission among the Cherokees. The New York Missionary Society sent its representative to visit the Chickasaws. In the printed report of the New York Society appeared the statement, dated from Knoxville, Tennessee: "The Cherokees who reside in the vicinity of Tennessee are desirous of having missionaries among them."

When this report was read in the annual meeting of the Society for Propagating the Gospel, at Salem, its effect was like an electric spark among the Brethren. Surely, at last the way was open! There followed earnest consideration of the matter and much discussion. Consultation of the lot gave approval of the appointment of Brother Abraham Steiner to visit the Cherokee chiefs. Christian Frederic de Schweinitz volunteered to go with him. On the night of October 28, 1799, a special service was held in the Salem Church with the whole congregation present when God's blessing was asked for the two Brethren setting out the next morning on their journey to the Cherokees.

After a long difficult journey on horseback, over rough mountain trails, the Brethren reached the Cherokee country in Eastern Tennessee only to find the chiefs gone on their annual hunting expedition. Despite their disappointment, the two made a wide tour of the "towns" and were kindly received by the Cherokees. Arts and crafts were being encouraged among them by United States agents, to promote civilization yet no provisions had been made for religious teaching. Colonel Buttler, the agent at Tellico, remembering the kindness of the people at Wachovia, extended every aid to the Brethren in their plans. Deeply interested in the welfare and progress of the Cherokees, he advised Brother Steiner to secure the consent of the chiefs before establishing a mission.

SPRINGPLACE

A year later during a second journey, Steiner and Schweinitz met the Upper Cherokee chiefs who consented to the establishment of the long hoped for mission. Through the influence of Charles Hicks, half Cherokee, an efficient interpreter in the employ of the Government, a location was made on the east side of the Connesauga River, the boundary between the Upper and the Lower Cherokee districts.

The site of the mission was in a beautiful location known as *Springplace*. Here were fine springs, plenty of limestone, hardwood timber, meadow land with good grass and clover and forty acres of red, fertile soil in cultivation. The right to occupy these premises was purchased by the Moravians from the former owner through James Vann, whose fine plantation home was two and a half miles away. Vann, half Cherokee, a wealthy trader and slaveholder, was the hospitable and generous friend of the Brethren during many difficulties in planting the mission.[8]

Having returnd to Salem, Brother Steiner, this time accompanied by young Gottlieb Byhan, set out on horseback with one pack horse loaded with supplies over the road four hundred miles to Springplace. After their arrival, it was three months before the owner was ready to vacate the farm, the two Brethren in the meantime planting and tending a crop and building a small cabin into which they moved on July 13, 1801. That same night their prayers were the dedication of the first mission station among the Cherokees. Hope and a vision of the work they were beginning were deep in their hearts as they read this text by the light of a pine torch that night: "I will make thy name to be remembered in all generations; therefore shall the people praise thee forever and ever."

Though the founder of Springplace Mission, ill health prevented Brother Steiner's earnest desire to make it his permanent residence. The first members regularly in charge were Jacob Wohlfahrt and his wife (Elizabeth Schneider), and Gottlieb Byhan and his bride (Dorothea Schneider).

The first mission school among the Cherokees was begun at Springplace in the spring of 1802, with Sally, James Vann's youngest daughter, and Polly Vann, her cousin, as pupils. The missionaries did not know the Cherokee language, a circumstance which greatly hampered their early mission work, much to their distress. Dissatisfied with the slow progress of

---

[8] The present town of Spring Place, Murray County, Georgia, is located on the site of Springplace Moravian Mission.

the school, the chiefs soon threatened to order the Brethren out of the nation. They had steadily refused the chief's wishes that twenty-five to thirty pupils be boarded and clothed free at the expense of the Moravian Church.[9] While truly missionary in spirit, the fundamental principle of the Church was to train the individual to depend upon his own efforts yet to be a willing helper for Christian service. Through the friendly assistance of Colonel Return J. Meigs, Cherokee agent, the time of trial for the mission was extended a year, one of the chiefs bringing in his eight-year-old son to attend the school, in the autumn of 1804. By Christmas, the meaning of the "Lovefeast" had been explained to the five Cherokee children in attendance who happily joined in singing the Christmas hymns in English.

From October, 1805, for a period of many years, Brother John Gambold and Mrs. Gambold were missionaries in charge of Springplace. They loved the Cherokees, making the first permanent mission in their midst the cradle of Christian civilization in this Indian nation.

Brother Gambold's optimism and purely consecrated spirit were the inspiration that advanced this cause. He had charge of all religious instruction and services besides temporal affairs, taking an active part in the labor of the mission home and farm. Every Moravian Brother was truly a missionary in spiritual matters; at the same time he was also skilled in some vocation either as carpenter, joiner, cooper, weaver, or shoemaker. Mission work included careful instruction and training of pupils and converts in Christian life, besides giving due attention to their temporal interests and needs which built up "the physical, moral, and spiritual life of the native community," thus making "its good influence contagious."

---

9 In 1803, a Presbyterian school was opened for 21 pupils among the Cherokees on the Hiwassee River, by Rev. Gideon Blackburn. The school was closed in 1810.

Mrs. Gambold had charge of the school at Springplace. She has been described as "sprightly in person as well as in fancy and imagination" with the gift of making the hearts of her Indian pupils "blossom like the rose." Her first Christmas at the mission, a few weeks after her coming, six children in the school under her direction sang "How shall I Meet My Savior?," each child carrying a real wax taper. They had helped to decorate the room with evergreens and a gilded inscription "Christ is Born!." Thus, many years before festivities had been made a usual part of the Christmas celebration in the States, these Cherokee girls and boys had learned old-time Moravian customs. Mrs. Gambold was a highly talented woman who had previously been for a number of years, principal of the Moravian Boarding school for young ladies in Bethlehem, Pennsylvania.

The day at Springplace began in winter at day break, in summer at sunrise, all up and dressed and kneeling in family prayer. Breakfast over, school was in session until dinner. The hours until late afternoon were spent by the girls and boys helping at their respective tasks, about the household and the farm, with some time allowed for play. Another session of school was followed by supper and evening songs and prayer before an early hour of retirement.

When the Gambolds came to Springplace, they brought with them a Negro slave woman, called Pleasant, purchased to help lighten the arduous household tasks of the Sisters in the mission. Moravian Mission dwellings and premises were always noted for spotless cleanliness and well kept appearance.

The year 1810 was one of great joy to the missionaries. The first Cherokee to make a request for baptism in the

Moravian Church was Mrs. James Vann.[10] The birthday of
the Church, August 13th, was chosen for this important event
at Springplace. The only building large enough to accommo-
date the crowd in attendance was the huge new barn which
had been beautifully decorated with green boughs and garlands of flowers. The following is a description of this
memorable occasion:

"The Candidate had spent most of the preceding night
in prayer. She was radiantly happy when the great morning
of her life dawned, and the light in her face on that morn
was prophetic of the Sun of Righteousness arising with heal-
ing in His wings upon the whole Cherokee Nation. Dressed
in white, she entered before the large congregation and the
service began. The school children sang heartily with their
teachers and Brother Gambold delivered a short, earnest address and poured out his heart in prayer to God for the Candidate, the whole assemblage, the entire Cherokee Nation.
Many persons wept during the service. Clearly and from her
heart Margaret answered the questions directed to every
Candidate for Baptism in the Moravian Church, whereupon
she knelt and was baptised by Brother Gambold, in the name
of the Father, the Son and the Holy Ghost, receiving the
name, Margaret Ann."

Another joyful time for the missionaries was in 1822
when Elias Boudinot, John Vann, John Ridge, and David
Taucheechy returned from school at Cornwall, Connecticut,
after completing several years of study there. They had
grown up to be fine young men and were looked upon

---

[10] Margaret Ann Vann was born on August 20, 1783, the daughter of
Walter Scott, a Scotchman, and his fullblood Cherokee wife. He had served
at one time as royal agent of the English, to the Cherokees. In 1809, occurred the great tragedy of the Springplace neighborhood in the murder of
James Vann as the result of a feud growing out of his duel with John Fall-
ing. The son of James and Margaret Ann Vann was Joseph Vann, born in
1800, better known as "Rich Joe" Vann. He moved to the Cherokee Nation,
West, and owned a large plantation near Webbers Falls on the Arkansas
River, in present Muskogee County, Oklahoma. Joseph Vann's daughter,
Delilah Amelia, attended Mount Holyoke Seminary in Massachusetts and
afterward married Oliver Hazard Perry Brewer. Their youngest son, O. H. P.
Brewer, Jr., was elected a member of the Constitutional Convention for the
State of Oklahoma. He is serving his second term as district judge at
Muskogee (1940).

THE LORD'S PRAYER IN CHEROKEE

.ᏫᏯᏓᏊ ᏌᏩᏣ ᏠᏗ ᏎᏓᏫᏗᏝ ᏋᎴᏗ ᏕᏋᏫᏘ ᏥᎡᏜᎦᏗ ᏣᏁ ᏅᏒᏛᏘ. ᏗᏂ ᏞᎦᏗ ᎾᏂᏌᏛᏫᏛ ᎠᏤᎾᎢᏝᏘ, ᎾᏯᏌ ᏌᏩᏣ ᏃᏂᏌᏟᏜ ᏝᏅᏝᏘᏤ ᎠᏌᏟᏛᏣᏗ ᏫᏯᎥ ᎪᎵ ᏘᎦ ᏕᎢᎾᏴᏘᏝᎥᏃ ᏎᎾᏴᏍᏘ, ᎾᏯᏌ ᏝᏗᏌᏒᏂᎢᏘ ᏣᏂᏍᏴ ᏓᏇ ᏞᏣᏗ ᏅᏣᏟᏉᏝᎦ ᏋᏘ ᏳᏝᎧᏴᏌᎣᏅᎳᏴᏴ. ᎾᏴᏣᏡᎦᎱᏝᏛᏍᎥ Ꮒ ᏃᏅ ᏋᏘᎢᏘ. ᏋᏟᏌᏃᏋ ᏥᎡᏜᎦᏗ ᏋᏘ, ᏗᏌ ᏎᏂᏴᏣᏗ ᏋᏘ, ᏗᏌ ᏞᎦᏌᏫᏗᏝ ᏋᏘ ᏂᎤᎾᏘ. ᏝᏅᏁᏨ.

INTERPRETATION, WITH PRONUNCIATION ACCORDING

TO THE ALPHABET.

aw gi daw·da | ga lv la di ehi | ga lv quo di yu | ge se
sdi | de tsa daw·vi | dsa gv wi yu hi ge sv | wi ga na nu
gaw i | a ni e law·hi | wi dsi ga li sda | ha da nv ste gv i |
na sgi ya | ga·lv la di | tsi'ni ga li sdi ha | ni da daw de
qui sv | aw ga li sda yv di | sgi v si | gaw hi i ga | di ge sgi
v si quo naw | de sgi du gv'i | na sgi ya | tsi di ga yaw tsi
na haw | tsaw tsi du gi | a le tla sdi | oo da'gaw le ye di yi
ge sv | wi di sgi ya ti nv sta nv gi | sgi yu da le sge sdi quo
sgi ni | oo yaw ge svi | tsa tse li ga ye naw | tsa gv wi yu
hi | ge sv i | a le | dsa li ni gi di yi | ge sv i | a le | e dsa lv
quo di yu | ge sv | ni gaw hi lv i | e me n.

TRANSLATION.

Our Father | heaven dweller, | Hallowed | be | thy
name. | Thy kingdom | let it make its appearance. | Here
upon earth | take place | Thy will, | the same as | in
heaven | [it] is done. | Daily [adj.] | our food give to us |
this day. | Forgive us | our debts, | the same as | we for-
give | our debtors. | And do not | temptation being | lead
us into [it]. | Deliver us from | evil existing. | For thine |
the kingdom | is. | and | the power | is. | and | the glory |
is, | forever | amen.

THE LORD'S PRAYER IN CHEROKEE TYPE
from Sequoyah's Alphabet, at top of page.

lovingly and with great pride by the Moravian missionaries. Having taught the boys in the mission at school at Springplace, they had made every effort to send them to Cornwall to complete their education.

Looking into the records and history of the Moravian Church in the nation, beginning with Springplace, one finds the names of many prominent Cherokees. Some of them, or their descendants, were leaders in their nation in Oklahoma. Early Cherokee members of the Moravian Church included Charles Renatus Hicks and his wife, Anna Felicitas;[11] Christian David Watie and his wife, Susanna Charity, parents of Elias Boudinot (or Buck Watie) and of General Stand Watie; Clement Vann and his wife, Mary Christiana, parents of James Vann; Susanna Catherine Ridge, wife of Major Ridge; William Abraham Hicks and his wife, Sarah Bithiah; Delilah McNair, wife of Captain David McNair; Mrs. Nancy Adair, Mrs. Susanna Fields, and others.

Many prominent persons were entertained at Springplace, including United States Government officials and noted scholars and scientists. In his tour of the United States, the

[11] In a conversation concerning the plans to civilize the Indian people, John Calhoun, Secretary of War, once stated: "We need never despair when we can show such evidence as Charles Hicks." Described as a "man of integrity, temperance and intelligence," Charles Hicks was long an outstanding leader in the nation, serving as second chief from about 1810 until a short time before his death. He died January 20, 1827, thirteen days after the death of Principal Chief Pathkiller, during which period Hicks served as principal chief. Having had a fair education in his youth, he diligently improved himself by reading in later life. Through his influence, the Cherokee National Council approved the first written law in the nation, in 1808. Several years before Sequoyah had completed his wonderful invention of the Cherokee alphabet, Charles Hicks gave much patient and persevering labor in making the first translation of the Lord's Prayer into Cherokee, for the Moravian Church, using as accurately as possible English letters for the Cherokee sounds. He was born on Dec. 23, 1767, at Thomaatly, on the Hiwassee River, the son of Nathan Hicks, a white trader, and his Cherokee wife, a daughter of Chief Broom. When he was baptised on April 16, 1813, as the second Cherokee convert of the Moravian Church, Charles Hicks received the middle name of "Renatus" (the *Renewed*), an old Moravian Church name.

Catholic Abbe, Correa de Serra, minister to the United States from Portugal, a distinguished naturalist and linguist, wrote enthusiastically of his visit at the mission:

"Judge of my surprise in the midst of the wilderness to find a botanic garden, not indeed like that at Paris, or yours at Kew; but a botanic garden, containing many exotic and medicinal plants, the professor, Mrs. Gambold, describing them by their Linnean names. Your missionaries have taught me more of the nature of the manner of promulgating civilization and religion in the early ages by the missionaries from Rome, than all the ponderous volumes which I have read on the subject. I there saw the sons of a Cherokee Regulus learning their lesson, and reading their Testament in the morning, and drawing and painting in the afternoon, though to be sure in a very Cherokee style; and assisting Mrs. Gambold in her household work or Mr. Gambold planting corn. Precisely so in the forests of Germany or France, a Clovis or a Bertha laid aside their crowns, and studied in the hut of a St. Martin or another missionary."

In 1826, Springplace Mission included a well kept farm and gardens, with several log houses built around a square set with china berry, catalpa, peach, apple, and cherry trees. A few steps from the main dwelling was the church with its tall belfry, from which the ringing of its clear toned bell could be heard many miles. Across the lane in front of the church, fine orchards were on either side of the cemetery in which lay the grave of Anna Rosina Gambold beside that of her Cherokee Sister, Margaret Ann Vann.

Christian missionaries among the Cherokees saw a long period of troubled days before the removal of the nation west. In 1821, a second Cherokee mission, called Oochgelogy, had been established by Brother Gambold four miles from New Echota. One day in 1831, Reverend Charles G. Clauder was quietly at work teaching the school at Oochgelogy when a company of the Georgia Guard rode up and arrested him. Leaving his wife and pupils weeping and terrified, he was taken to the Guard headquarters where he explained that instructions from the Moravian Society at Salem forbade his remaining among the Cherokees unless he could carry on his missionary work. He was allowed to return to his grief stricken family and pupils, though ten days later came the final warning from Georgia authorities that he must leave the mission within ten days.[12]

Springplace was also lost when the Cherokee lands were distributed by lottery, the white claimants coming in and rudely demanding the mission houses, fields, and other property, in 1833. Captain David McNair, who was the friend of every Christian denomination, offered the Moravian missionaries residence at his place across the line in Tennessee, eighteen miles from Springplace. This was the temporary location of the Moravian work until the removal of the Cherokees to the West. During this tragic time, scattered groups of Cherokee members of the Church lived exemplary lives. In the neighborhood of Oochgelogy, George Hicks and Christian David Watie held prayer meetings regularly and church services every Sunday until after the signing of the Cherokee Removal Treaty at New Echota, in 1835.

NEW SPRINGPLACE

Appointed by the Moravian Society to go to the Indian Territory to select a location for a new Cherokee mission, Miles Vogler and Herman Reude, accompanied by Reverend Johan Renatus Schmidt, set out overland from Eastern Ten-

---

12 The missions had been founded and supported by the Moravian Society through the limited donations from the Salem Church, from a few special patrons, and from a special bequest in 1825. In 1809, the sum of $100.00 a year was first granted from an Indian ciivlization fund appropriated by the United States, ten years later increased to $250.00 a year. These sums seemed large and were received with great rejoicing by the missionaries, for the help had come when money and supplies were at the vanishing point in the missions. Through the Government's policy of allowing any religious organization payment for its mission property in the East, the Moravian Society received the net amount of $6,441.33, about two years after the signing of the Treaty at New Echota, for its holdings at Springplace and Oochgelogy, which sum was held in trust by the Society for replanting the work in the West.

nessee in a small wagon, driving a team of horses. They crossed the line into the Indian Territory on October 27, 1838, having made the eight hundred mile journey in forty-one days, by way of Nashville, thence through Kentucky, Southern Illinois, Missouri, and on to Fayetteville, Arkansas.

By chance when stopping at an inn one night, after crossing the Territorial line, the travelers rejoiced to meet Thomas Watie, a former pupil of Brother Schmidt at Spring-place, one of the sons of Christian David Watie. The young man accompanied the Brethren as a guide to the Barren Fork where several Cherokee families, members of the Moravian Church, had formed a settlement through the aid of their friend, General Matthew Arbuckle, Commandant at Fort Gibson.[13]   On the way, the Brethren visited Park Hill Mission where they were warmly welcomed by their old friend, Reverend Samuel A. Worcester.

At the Barren Fork settlement, the Cherokees had cleared ten acres for the site of a mission and a part of the ground had been planted in wheat. In the clearing near good springs, two cabins, a corn crib, and a blacksmith shop had been built. With a permit from the United States Agent to settle any place in the nation that they might select, the Brethren purchased these improvements for $550.00, moving into their new quarters by Christmas, 1838. Twenty Chero-kee communicants of the Moravian Church lived near as neighbors.

Life in the new settlement was truly pioneer. Log cabins were small, furniture and all equipment crude, with food generally limited to corn meal and salt pork. Even these supplies were hard to buy. In the summer of 1839, an epi-

---

[13] Barren Fork Mission was near the present village of Proctor, at the mouth of Tiner's Creek on the Barren Fork River, present Adair County, Oklahoma.

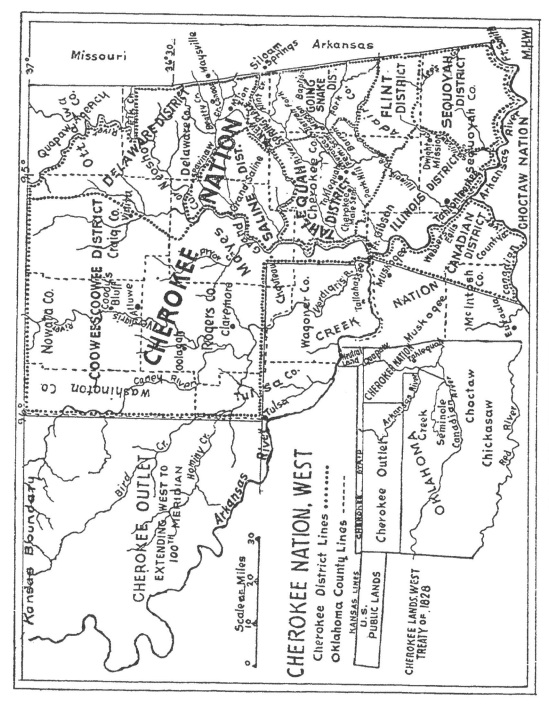

MAP OF CHEROKEE NATION, WEST.
Organized districts to 1907, indicated by dotted lines. Inset map showing location of Cherokee lands in Oklahoma, Treaty of 1828.

demic of malarial fever swept the community, with no medicine on hand and a physician many miles away. On account of the unhealthful location, several Cherokee families moved to Beattie's Prairie forty miles north of Barren Fork Mission, a number of Moravian Church members having already settled in this second location. Through the recommendation of Chief John Ross, the National Council named Beattie's Prairie as the location of the Moravian Mission.[14]

In 1840, a few improvements were purchased here by the Brethren and additions immediately begun. A short time after Brother Volger and his wife (Dorothea Reude) settled at Beattie's Prairie, they were honored by a visit from John Howard Payne on a tour of the Indian Territory. The Cherokees helped to build a schoolhouse in a beautiful grove of oaks near a fine spring. School was opened in September, 1840, with seven pupils in attendance and Brother Herman Reude as teacher. So successful was the work that a number of families in the neighborhood, mostly half Cherokee and non-church members, soon subscribed funds and a second school building was erected. Mrs. Vogler opened this school for girls in May, 1841, Brother Reude continuing as teacher of the boys. Brother Vogler conducted Bible instruction, holding regular church services at several places besides Beattie's Prairie and Barren Fork forty miles south.

Church services held at Spring Creek by some Cherokee members roused much interest. A call was made for the organization of a church and school at this point, twenty-one miles south on the road from Beattie's Prairie to Barren Fork. With the wholehearted interest of Chief Ross and the approval of the National Council, the Moravian Brethren erected a schoolhouse and a mission residence at Spring Creek,

---

[14] In 1845, the name of Beattie's Prairie Mission was changed to *Canaan.* The location was in present Delaware County, five miles west of the village of Maysville, Arkansas.

during the summer of 1842. The mission was called *New Springplace* in memory of Springplace in the former Cherokee homeland.[15]

Brother Vogler held the dedication services in the church and school building at New Springplace on September 11, 1842. A week later, school was opened with twenty-one pupils in attendance and Brother Gilbert Bishop as teacher. He had made an alphabet of large wooden letters and Chief Ross had brought a trunk full of books from the Church at Bethlehem where he had recently visited on a journey east. Many of the pupils at New Springplace were young men and women eager to learn, though some of them had never attended school.

As the years passed, the work of the Moravian Church in Cherokee Nation centered at Springplace.[16] Church members increased and there was great interest in the schools. Withal there were deep shadows over life in the new country. There were droughts when crops failed and springs dried up, water having to be hauled in kegs from the creeks. There were floods when crops were washed away. Then famine threatened. Every season sickness was prevalent—malaria, pneumonia, and epidemics.

With the increasing settlement of the West, the organization of Kansas and Nebraska territories in 1854, and the promotion of transcontinental railroad building, covetous eyes were again cast on Indian lands as they had been east of the Mississippi a generation before. In a radical speech

---

[15] New Springplace Mission was located a half mile west of the present village of Oaks, in Delaware County, Oklahoma.

[16] In 1845, the Presbyterian mission station at Mt. Zion, six miles south of Canaan, was taken over by the Moravians at the request of Rev. D. S. Buttrick, Presbyterian missionary, who had to resign his work on account of ill health. In addition to the regular mission stations, Moravian Church members held services in their homes in isolated communities in the Cherokee Nation.

made in the North, a politician stated in effect that *the Indian Territory south of Kansas must be cleared of all the Indians.* Agitation of the anti-slavery question was growing in the North. Controversies and animosities arising from these movements in the United States were cause for alarm among the Indian people in the Indian Territory. Some of the great church organizations in America were disrupted along sectional lines, the missionaries and mission work among the Indians bearing the consequences. The Moravian Church was opposed to slavery as an institution, taking the stand of neutrality on public and political questions of the day, devoting itself to spiritual and educational matters and the immediate temporal needs of the Church communities. Such had been the ideals of the Moravian Church for nearly a thousand years.

The Mission Conference at New Springplace on November 1, 1858, brought fresh inspiration and renewed efforts in the Moravian missions. It was at this meeting that James Ward was received as an Acolyte in the service of the Church, chosen as secretary of the Conference. Both he and his wife, Esther Hoyt Ward, were of Cherokee descent and had recently become members of the Moravian Church. Having been a student at Dartmouth College and having served successfully as an instructor in the Cherokee national schools, James Ward had been appointed by the Society at Salem as missionary teacher at New Springplace. Reverend Gilbert Bishop and Archie Henry, interpreter, were also on the mission staff. In the Church report from the Conference, Mr. Ward was specially mentioned as "a sincere and promising Brother who devotes himself to his duties with his whole soul."

A large building had been erected and specially dedicated for church services at New Springplace, in 1849. Just ten years later, a new schoolhouse had been completed and was dedicated at the Lovefeast on September 28, 1859, to the service of Christian education. Brother Ward was teacher, attendance was increasing, and the school was popular in the community.

In the midst of this progress that gave hope and faith for a greater future in the Church and school came the clouds of war between the States. The tragic death of James Ward on September 2, 1862, brought the close of New Springplace Mission for many years. It was the bright promise which his life had given that became the inspiration for this memorial story of the Moravian Church among the Cherokees.

PART III

THE MISSIONARY WARDS

John Ward

In 1764, John ("Jack") Ward, a native of Ireland, leaving the ship on which he had sailed to America, set out for the Cherokee country. Arriving at Echota, he learned that his father, Brian Ward, for whom he was seeking, had separated from his Cherokee wife, Nancy Ward, and no longer lived in the Cherokee country.[17]

Brian Ward had served in the British army during the colonial wars in America. He was a descendant of the Irish nobility and was a relative of an officer in the British army, by the name of Ward. When his military service ended, his wife having died in Ireland, Brian Ward became a trader among the Cherokees. Under a tribal law instituted at an early date, no white man could remain permanently in the

---

[17] In the battle between the Cherokee forces of the war chief, Oconostota, and the Creeks at Taliwa, Northern Georgia, in 1755, an incident occurred, important in the history of the Cherokees: Nancy, the daughter of Chief Attakullaculla's sister of the Wolf Clan, was the wife of the warrior, Kingfisher, of the Deer Clan. Having accompanied her husband to help him during the fight with the Creeks, she was lying back of a log chewing lead bullets to make them more effective in rifle fire when he was killed in the battle. Instantly seizing his rifle, she fought on with his Cherokee comrades. For her part in the battle, she was given a Negro slave from the spoils of war, thus becoming the first slaveholder in her nation. Her second husband was Brian Ward. From this time, she was known as Nancy Ward.

Nancy Ward's bravery and valor in the battle at Taliwa subsequently won her the election of *Ghigua* or *Beloved Woman* in her nation. During the war of the American Revolution, she lived at Echota. Loyal to the Americans, she warned the frontier settlements of attacks planned by the warring Cherokees and at one time saved the life of the American captive, Mrs. Bean. Though famous for her grace and poise, Nancy Ward's business talent won for her wealth in slaves and stock. It was said that she was the first to introduce the raising of cattle into the Cherokee country. In her old age, when unable to attend the national councils, she sent her walking cane and her vote on important questions. In the Cherokee Council at Amoah, May 6, 1817, she thus voted the renunciation of her high office as *Beloved Woman* in favor of written constitutional law.

Nancy Ward's given name was no doubt the Anglicized form of her Cherokee name *Nanye'hi*. This was an old personal name among the Cherokees, signifying "One who goes about," from *Nunne'hi*, the legendary name of the spirit people in Cherokee myth.

Cherokee country and have the protection of the Cherokee chiefs unless he married into the tribe and made his home in the tribal domain.

John Ward found his stepmother, Nancy Ward, the most influential woman among her people, the Cherokees. She was wealthy in her own right and was highly respected both by them and the Americans, in her position as the *Ghigua* or *Beloved Woman* in her nation. She and her first husband, Kingfisher, who was killed in the battle at Taliwa, in 1755, had two children, Catherine and Fivekiller. Nancy and her second husband, Brian Ward, had one daughter, Elizabeth Ward, a half sister to John Ward.

John remained in the Cherokee country and married Catherine McDaniel, best known in her family at "Katie." She was the seventeen year old daughter of a Scotchman named McDaniel and his fullblood Cherokee wife, called "Granny Hopper."[18]

[18] The old English records of colonial authorities, before 1765, referred to the principal chief or "emperor" of the Cherokees as "Old Hop." His Cherokee name was sometimes spelled *Kanagatucko*, in the records. One authoritative writer concerning the Cherokees has stated that this name was a combination with the Cherokee word *"okou"* (or *u'guku*) meaning "owl," a high title in the old tribal government.

James Ward, Sr.

James Ward, sr., was born on October 22, 1785, the eldest son of John and Catherine ("Katie") Ward. This period was a dangerous time. Cherokee warriors were provoked into raiding the settlements in Tennessee. American volunteer troops under Robertson and Sevier destroyed Cherokee "towns" and property.

One early day writer on the Cherokees gave the following description, illustrating the cruel reprisals on the frontier at that time:

"The Cherokee Chief, Oconostota, resigned the chieftaincy on account of old age, in 1782, and was succeeded by Tassel. Oconostota, or "Ground hog sausage," as his name was translated, died in 1785. Tassel was a well known friend of the whites. In 1788, he was invited to the headquarters of Major James Hubbert. He accepted the invitation and visited the headquarters with his son and two members of his tribe. As soon as they were within his lines, Hubbert had them conveyed to a vacant house and placing a tomahawk in the hands of a young man whose parents had been killed by a marauding band of Cherokees, told him to kill all of the visiting Cherokees, which he did while the Major stood guard at the door."

This was the only instance of a head chief of the Cherokees being killed or murdered, except one time in the case of a Texas Cherokee chief.

Scattered throughout the Cherokee country were Scotch, Irish, German, and English settlers who had married into the tribe, as had McDaniel, Adair, John Ward, Clement Vann, Daniel Ross, George Lowry, sr., and others.

James Ward's character and ability proved that he had inherited the hardy spirit of his father and mother. In his mature years, he settled in Georgia where he became a respected plantation owner. His first wife, Sarah Redding, died soon after their marriage. His second wife was Lucy Hainy and they were the parents of ten children.

James Ward, Sr., moved to the Indian Territory during the time of the removal of the Cherokees from Georgia. His business affairs had prospered. He was the owner of extensive plantations and many Negro slaves. Arriving in the Territory, he selected a favorable location for his new plantation home and was prospering again in the nation west, before many seasons. The Ward Family Bible recorded his death, "May 20th, 1859, in the 74th year of his age. *I am prepared to die.*"

James Ward, Jr.

James Ward, Jr., was born on November 15, 1826, the son and namesake of James Ward, Sr., and his wife, Lucy Hainy. The son was only a lad when the great tragedy of the "Trail of Tears" occurred, the Cherokees having been driven from their homes at the points of soldiers' bayonets. Most of the emigrants were fullbloods, though many hundreds were of a small degree of Cherokee blood, even more loyal—if words can describe their feelings—to their Indian friends, kinsmen, and nation.

As a youth, James was given every advantage of schooling afforded in the unsettled conditions of early days in the West. When he reached his majority, his father offered to give him some slaves and establish him that he might make his own living.

"Father, I wish you would give me the money instead," replied James. "I want to go to college. I should like to prepare in my studies at Dwight and then go to Dartmouth College."

Greatly pleased with his son, Mr. Ward furnished him with the necessary money and sent him off to Dwight Mission. At that time, Dwight offered schooling in the elementary and high school studies. Moved west from its original site in Arkansas, by the American Board of Commissioners, this Presbyterian school was attended by youths of leading Cherokee families at their own expenses for board and school supplies. Through the interest and influence of Reverend Worcester Willey, Superintendent of Dwight Mission, James was recommended and admitted to Dartmouth College, attending in 1852-53. On account of increasing anti-slavery sentiment in the North, southern boys whose families were slave owners began leaving the northern colleges and schools.

JAMES WARD, Jr.

After returning to the Cherokee Nation, James Ward, Jr., the handsome, fair haired young Cherokee, married Miss Esther Hoyt, also of Cherokee descent, a teacher at Park Hill. She was of distinguished ancestry on both sides of her family. Her paternal grandfather was Reverend Ard Hoyt, missionary of the American Board to the Cherokees. Her maternal grandfather was Major George Lowry, veteran leader and assistant principal chief of the Cherokee Nation.

Major George Lowry

Major George Lowry was born in 1770, the second of seven children of George Lowry, Sr., a native of Scotland, and Nancy, the fullblood Cherokee daughter of *Oo-lu-tsa* ("She's come"). The Cherokee name of George, jr., was *Agi'li* ("He is rising"), the contraction of an old Cherokee name *Agin-Agi'li* ("Rising-fawn").

Major Lowry was one of the great leaders of the Cherokee Nation, during the critical period of its development as a republic, thirty years that saw the establishment of its constitutional government, its immigration to the Indian Territory, and its founding as a nation west. For many years up to about 1820, he was town chief of Willstown, Cherokee Nation (in Eastern Alabama), a position that was hereditary under the old tribal form of government.

He signed his name to many important documents in Cherokee history. One of these was the *Compact,* negotiated around the "Great Council Fire" at Tahlequah, in the summer of 1843, establishing lasting "Peace and Friendship," and signed by elected representatives of the Cherokees, Creeks, and Osages. This document was published as a law of the Cherokee Nation. It marked a milestone in the history of these three great Indian nations that had been long been enemies and fought many battles with one another under their ancient tribal regimes. The successful accomplishment

of this measure was largely due to the influence and efforts
of Major Lowry during the noted intertribal council at Tahlequah.   Elected master of ceremonies, this venerable leader,
at that time 73 years old, explained the symbolism of the
wampum, pipe, and tobacco used in the old Indian peace
councils.   The throng of more than four thousand Indians,
many of them the official delegates of twenty-one nations
and tribes, was the largest convened in the early history of
Tahlequah and did much to promote friendly acquaintance
and peaceful relations in the Southwest.

William P. Ross, Cherokee leader and editor of "The
Cherokee Advocate," published at Tahlequah, wrote the fol-
lowing tribute to his lifelong friend and compatriot, Major
George Lowry:

"The greatness of Major Lowry was not of that type of
heroism that, flashing like the meteor or like the glowing
comet, challenges admiration for some individual acts of
prowess or skillful manipulation of some stirring event, to
weave from necessities of many garlands for the individual
brow, but his appears to have been a life of unwavering de-
votion to the principles of recitude and truth. He was noted
for truthfulness; his word esteemed good as his oath; his
promise equal to his bond. Physically he was tall, well
developed and of dignified carriage.   An approachable man
even by children, and yet not a man likely to be treated
with disrespect by any.   Not perfectly free in the use of the
English language, he had no superior in the use of his own.
His diction was considered the best, always clear and free
from ambiguities.   His public career runs through the most
eventful history of the Cherokee people, from the adoption
of the costume and habits of civilized life down to the period
of his death on October 20th, 1852.

"Before he had reached the years of maturity, he was
employed by an officer of the army to carry a dispatch to a

commander in Canada, which he accomplished, traversing that then vast wilderness on foot, successfully eluding all enemies, both going and returning.

"The title of Major was not merely an honorary one, but one gained by faithful military service under Gen. Jackson, during the war of 1812. At that time he lived north in Tennessee on Battle Creek, or Niccojack Cove. . . . Several of his children attended the mission school at Brainerd and he and his wife, Lucy Benge, were early members of the mission church (Presbyterian). On the organization of the Willstown Presbyterian church, he was installed one of the ruling elders, an office he sustained with zeal and fidelity until the removal of the people west in 1838-39. After the removal, the churches having been reorganized as Congregational churches, he was chosen one of the deacons of the Park Hill church, which position he held at the time of his death.

"Major Lowry was ever an active friend of, and earnest co-worker with, missionaries. Especially were his services invaluable as an interpreter. . . . The Bible was his constant study. The prophecies of Isaiah were greatly admired and portions were translated by him into the Cherokee language.

"After the death of Principal Chief Hicks, it was desired by many to place him in that position, but he magnanimously declined in favor of one deemed more competent in many respects to fill the office, and was placed in the second position, that of assistant principal chief and executive adviser. In this capacity he served his nation for most of the time during thirty years, frequently serving as principal chief, as required by the constitution, during the absence of the principal chief.

"The National Council which was in session at the time of his death, demanded the chief mourner's place. His re-

mains were taken from his residence to the capitol of the
Cherokee Nation, where by invitation of the council, Rev.
S. A. Worcester delivered a funeral discourse in the presence
of both branches of the national council, members of the
executive department and other officers, and many citizens
of the Cherokee Nation. The estimation in which the de-
ceased was held by the pastor, the veteran missionary Worcester, who knew him well for so many years, and so little
disposed to flattery, might be in some measure judged by the
text selected as the theme of his remarks on that occasion—
"And he did that which was right in the sight of the Lord."
His remains rest in the national cemetery at Tahlequah,
marked by an appropriate but unpretentious monument."

This monument bears the following inscriptions on four
sides:

"George Lowery, Born at Tahskeegee on Tennessee River
about 1770. Died October 20, 1852, Age 82 years.

"Erected by order of the National Council.

"Many years member of the Church of Christ. Ruling
Elder of the Church at Willstown, Deacon of the Church at
Park Hill. He fulfilled the duties of every office well. An
honest man, A Spotless Patriot, A Devoted Christian.

"Visited President Washington as a delegate for the
Cherokee Nation 1791 or 92. Captain of the Lighthorse 1810.
Member of First National Committee of 1814. One of the
delegation who negotiated the Treaty of 1819. Member of
the Committee who formed the Constitution of 1827. Also
that of 1839. Elected Assistant Principal Chief 1828 and often
afterwards. At his death a member of Executive Council.
Filled various other public offices."

LYDIA LOWRY

In the summer of 1816, while on a visit to Washington
in the interests of his people, Chief George Lowry, of Willstown, met and conversed with Reverend Cyrus Kingsbury,
appointed by the American Board of Commissioners of

Foreign Missions (Presbyterian, Dutch Reformed, Congregational) to begin a mission among the Cherokees. As a result, a lifelong friendship was established and the first mission of the American Board was planted among the people of this nation. The mission was called *Brainerd*, located on the east side of Chickamauga Creek in Eastern Tennessee, two miles from the Georgia line. From its founding in 1817, Brainerd flourished as the largest mission of the American Board among the southeastern Indians, noted for its school and its wide influence for Christian civilization. In keeping with the spirit of both institutions, the missionaries at Brainerd held the Moravian Brethren in close friendship and often visited Springplace.

An old record of Brainerd makes special mention of "Lydia Lowry, the pious and intelligent daughter" of Chief George Lowry and his wife, Lucy Benge Lowry. Lydia was sixteen years old when she joined the Presbyterian Church and was baptised at Brainerd on January 31, 1819. Soon afterward in a dream, thoughts came to her so clearly in beautiful words that upon rising the next morning she wrote them down as the first hymn by a Cherokee.

In February, 1820, Lydia was married to Milo Hoyt, a former student at Princeton and the son of Reverend Ard Hoyt, missionary at Brainerd. Early that spring, through the earnest request of John Ross, a school was established at Willstown, on the Chatooga River, in Eastern Alabama. On April 3, Milo and Lydia Hoyt set out from Brainerd traveling the fifty mile journey over the mountains and south to Lydia's old home and the new mission station, Milo to be employed as teacher. Their first residence was a small log cabin near which the Cherokees immediately began to build the school-house.

Some years later, Milo Hoyt studied to be a physician and in his profession served in the Union Brigade, under the command of Colonel William A. Phillips, early in the war between the states. Many descendants of three Hoyt brothers who had come from England to America in colonial times rose to positions of prominence, some serving as officials in the States.

Reverend Ard Hoyt was pastor of the Presbyterian Church at Wilkesbarre, Pennsylvania, when he volunteered for missionary work among the Cherokees in 1817, arriving at Brainerd the next year. He was born at Danbury, Connecticut, on October 23, 1770. Mrs. Hoyt (Esther Booth) was born at Southbury, Connecticut, on January 18, 1774. Reverend Hoyt died at Willstown on February 18, 1828. Mrs. Ard Hoyt continued in the mission service until 1834.

Esther Hoyt

Esther Hoyt was born at Willstown, on March 18, 1826, the daughter of Dr. Milo and Lydia (Lowry) Hoyt. As a child she knew the tragic days of her people leaving their homelands east of the Mississippi. She also knew the inspiration and the joy of living in the new country of the Cherokees in the West. The activities of her venerable grandfather, Major Lowry, in the affairs of the nation were her interest and her life as a young girl. In keeping with the ideals and the character of her family, she, too, made her contribution in service for the advancement of Christian civilization. As a young woman, she taught in the Park Hill Mission, whose superintendent was the noted Reverend Samuel A. Worcester, veteran missionary to the Cherokees.

James and Esther Ward

After their marriage on February 9, 1854, James and Esther (Hoyt) Ward made their first home at Beattie's Prairie, in the neighborhood of Canaan Mission. Though James was a Methodist and his wife a Presbyterian, they had many lifelong friends among the Moravian Church members.

ESTHER HOYT WARD

The Methodist Episcopal Church had divided along
sectional lines, over the slavery question, in 1845, and a
similar move threatened the Presbyterian Church, seriously
hampering the work of these great religious organizations.
In April, 1858, Mr. and Mrs. Ward joined the Moravian
Church. Soon afterward, the Society at Salem, N. C., appointed him assistant missionary to Reverend Gilbert Bishop
at New Springplace. Having taught successfully in the
Cherokee schools, Brother Ward served as the teacher of the
school at the mission station. Of his ability and character,
Reverend Bishop later wrote in praise: "He was well fitted
for his duties as a teacher and zealous in the discharge of
the same; as a Christian he set a good example to his people,
and as my associate he was affable and friendly."

From 1858, Mr. and Mrs. Ward made New Springplace
their home.[19] As a member of a southern family, James
Ward's sympathies were with the Confederate States at the
outbreak of the war between the states. He remained faithful
to the trust imposed in him as a missionary of the Moravian
Church, which had always opposed participation of its members in war and had taken a neutral position in view of the
impending conflict. It took bravery and courage for James
Ward to remain carrying on his profession and spreading
Christian faith in the community at Springplace. Being
Cherokee and naturally sympathetic with their relatives and
friends, the bitter strife that sundered the Cherokee Nation
from the beginning of the War was especially dangerous for
Mr. Ward and his wife.

In 1859, the secret society of the Keetoowah organized
by Reverend Evan Jones and his son, John B. Jones, Baptist
missionaries, among the fullblood Cherokees, strongly sup-

---

19 About 1856, James Ward joined the Masonic Lodge at Maysville, Arkansas, as a charter member.

ported the cause of abolitionism. Within their own nation, the Keetoowahs were generally opposed to the mixed blood Cherokees and slaveholders. During the War, members of the Keetoowah served in the Union Army. Employed as scouts, they were known as "Cherokee Pins," from their Keetoowah insignia, two pins crossed on the left coat lapel.

At the outbreak of the War in the United States, feeling in the Cherokee Nation divided along the lines of the old feud of 1839 and subsequent party strife, Stand Watie and his followers of the *Ridge Party* taking up the cause of the Confederacy, while members of the *Ross Party* favored the Federal Government. Chief John Ross continued to urge a neutral course for his nation and furthered the cause throughout the Indian Territory, among other nations and tribes.

The first week in May, 1861, came the stroke that decided subsequent events in this part of the Southwest. By order of the Federal Military department in Kansas, all Federal troops were withdrawn to Fort Leavenworth, in that state, leaving the Indian Territory open ground for war. On May 13, the whole Territory was organized as a part of the Confederate Military department in the Southwest, with Brig.-Gen. Ben McCulloch, of Texas, in command. Fort Gibson, hardly forty miles southwest of New Springplace, became headquarters for the Confederate forces and the main point for attack and capture by Federal troops from the north.

During the summer and fall of 1861, treaties were negotiated and signed by the Confederate Commissioner, Albert Pike, with the Indian nations and several western tribes, even John Ross having to give up his plans for neutrality and sign the Cherokee treaty with the Confederate States. The first fighting in the Indian Territory occurred in November and December, in which Confederate Indian troops and Texans attacked over five thousand Creeks and Seminoles, followers of Opothleyahola, who had remained loyal to the Union and were taking their families north seeking safety in Kansas. In these battles, many Cherokees of the Confederate Army refused to fight their former Indian neighbors and friends. From this time, these Cherokees, most of whom were "Pins," were open in their support of the Union and many of them were later members of the Indian Home Guard Brigade, in the Federal Army.

Federal troops made their first invasion from Kansas into the Indian Territory early in the summer of 1862. The expedition resulted in failure. On the retreat, Chief Ross and his family were escorted north where they remained during the War.

A large force of Federal troops, including the First and the Third Indian Home Guard Regiments, under the command of General James G. Blunt, were again on their way south from Kansas to Fort Gibson late in the summer of 1862. Real war had come to the Cherokee Nation with its people hopelessly divided in their loyalties and their aims. Fighting by guerilla bands was the order of the day. Advance Federal scouting parties of *Cherokee Pins*, minds inflamed with hatred and revenge, rode hard through the country around the Confederate lines and encampments, striking when they could.

During this hazardous time, James Ward remained steadily at his post as assistant missionary at New Springplace. He and his wife were now the parents of five children: Darius, Lydia, Clara, and infant twins, Henry and William.

One day in August after a hard day's work threshing wheat by tramping it, the old method of driving horses over it, the Negro hired man turned the horses into the pasture. At that moment four Cherokee Pins rode up to him. Having announced that they were on the lookout for James Ward to kill him for his Confederate sympathies, they caught two of the best horses in the pasture and rode off with them. Much alarmed, Brother Bishop urged Mr. Ward to hitch up a team and the wagon and take his wife and children to safety at Siloam Springs, about fifteen miles east across the Arkansas line where the young Brother's relatives lived. He said that he was not afraid and that he would remain to help Brother Bishop and his family in case of trouble. A week later, the four other work horses were stolen. Bishop's thirteen year old son, Edwin, asked the Negro man to loan his own horse to Mr. Ward that he might make up a team with his saddle horse and take Mrs. Ward and the children to safety. Thoroughly frightened by the threat of the "Pins" who said that they would kill him if he told their intentions against James Ward, the Negro flatly refused the request.

Toward evening on September 2, 1862, Mr. Ward saddled up his horse as usual to ride out and bring in the milk cows. His seven year old son, Darius, begged to go with him but was told that he could not that evening. Darius watched his father stand listening nearly a minute by his horse. Then quickly vaulting into the saddle, Ward rode off toward the creek at a brisk trot. He had hardly gone out of sight when a volley of shots sounded through the woods down by the creek.

Less than five minutes later, a party of twenty to thirty Cherokee Pins, with their faces painted to disguise themselves, surrounded James Ward's house. While his frightened family huddled together on the porch, the Indians led by one who seemed to know the premises proceeded to rob the house.[20] When the leader had taken all he wanted, he came to the door and spoke in Cherokee to Mrs. Ward, telling her to get ready to go with his men. She soon accompanied them away from her home, carrying her infant twins in her arms. She had been refused the privilege of taking Lucinda, the Negro maid, to help her. Brother Bishop was also taken prisoner with the promise that he would soon be allowed to return to his family.

Riding horseback Mrs. Ward and Mr. Bishop were taken away, arriving after nightfall at a point about seven miles from New Springplace where a Federal officer, a white man, awaited them and his Cherokee scouts. Some three weeks later, *The Moravian,* a Church paper in the States, published a letter dated September 8th, from Reverend Gilbert Bishop at Fort Scott, Kansas, telling his story of the tragedy at Springplace and the distressing conditions in the Cherokee Nation. The letter read:

"I have been forced to leave my post of Springplace, about 75 miles distant.

"On the 2nd of September, a few hours before dark, a command of Federal Cherokees rode up and requested me to go with them, about seven miles to where a white officer over them was awaiting me to speak with me. Mrs. Ward was also required to go.

"Several gunshots which were fired before the men rode up, convinced me that Mr. Ward my associate, must probably be killed, and by the next morning a friend disclosed to me that he was killed. Our poor brother fell thus at his post, and should be honored in that he wished to share the com-

---

[20] Darius recognized the voice of the leader and told his mother that he was Jesse Henry. She immediately recognized him. Jesse Henry had often stayed at the Wards' home and was familiar with the house and premises. In about 1871, he died, it was said, of remorse for the death of James Ward, having made confession of his part in the tragedy at Springplace to John B. Jones, the Baptist missionary. After the War, Jesse Henry became a preacher in the Baptist Church and was a member of the Cherokee National Council at the time of his death.

mon danger with me. By the mercy of God, through the favor of the Cherokee people, who would not harm their white missionary, they carried me off to put me in safety. * * * When I left it was thought I could return again, but the officer forbid it, on the ground of the safety of the women and children who were congregated in great numbers when I was taken.

"Sister Bishop and all the children with Mrs. Ward are yet, I hope, at Springplace. My request to Sr. Ward was that she should move into the house with Sr. Bishop, and not leave the place till I could come to their relief, which I hope to do, when the regiments move south again, as is expected, in a few weeks.

"They have enough flour and meal for a few weeks, if it is not taken from them. I see no prospect of our remaining at our post, but shall be guided by circumstances directing us to ascertain the will of the Lord.

"With the armies occupying and consuming the country, it can hardly fail to bring on a famine by winter and spring, and I cannot consent to let my family be led about in camp as fugitives.

"Between the armies about Springplace and Tahlequah, the country is already nearly laid waste. There are thousands of women and children coming or already here, and the government has to feed and sustain them."

As for the tragic experiences of Mrs. Ward, the story of this brave and courageous Cherokee mother should be ranked with those of the greatest heroes of her nation.

Leaving the Federal encampment, Mrs. Ward was conducted by the Cherokee scouts to a point about twenty miles from New Springplace. Here she was left alone in the wilderness, with her babes in her arms. Without food or help of any kind, she managed to make her way on foot, carrying the two four months old infants, and finally stumbled into her home almost dead. She had been away all the night of September 2nd, the next day and that night, and well up into the day of September 4th. She reported that Brother Bishop was in the guard tent of the Federal Army.

Though James Ward's death was strongly suspected, there had been no effort to search for him. There were no men folk at Springplace and one could only remain near the house in these dangerous hours. Feeling certain that her husband had been killed, Mrs. Ward accompanied by Mrs. Bishop and Edwin set out to search for Mr. Ward's remains, some hours after her return. On the bank of the Creek, his bunch of keys was discovered. Near at hand where the underbrush was beaten down, Edwin found the skeleton scattered about, with the legs still encased in boots, the flesh of the body having been devoured by buzzards and hogs and wolves. Edwin ran back to his house and soon returned to the fatal spot with a box and a wheelbarrow. After all the remains that could be found were placed in the box, it was nailed shut. Then, almost overcome with grief and fatigue, Esther Ward returned home, Mrs. Bishop walking sadly at her side and Edwin pushing the loaded wheelbarrow. Late that same evening, he went alone to the cemetery some distance away and began digging the grave.

The next morning Mrs. Ward and her five children and Mrs. Bishop and her six children formed the funeral procession to the cemetery. Mrs. Bishop read the funeral service and prayer was offered for the soul of James Ward.

Knowing the danger of remaining at New Springplace, Mrs. Ward and Mrs. Bishop decided to leave with their children as soon as possible for Siloam Springs, Arkansas. Many years afterward, Edwin Bishop wrote the following account of their journey:

"We made Hildebrant's mill the first day and stayed there over night. There was an empty house recently vacated, which we used for a temporary lodging. The next morning as we left the small settlment, Mr. Hildebrant gave us a hundred pound sack of flour. This we could not pay for at the moment, but the miller was sure that my father would pay him whenever he could.

"We made as much haste as possible, for we hoped to make Siloam Springs by nightfall. For a mile or two outside of Hildebrant's Mill our way was uphill. Our oxen team was strong and faithful with a never faltering tread. These oxen were the only livestock we had been able to bring with us.

"As we topped the rise, we noticed some riders coming toward us from Siloam Springs. It was a group of ten or twelve men from the Springs who had heard of Mr. Ward's death and were coming to investigate the matter. They were all Southerners and hard men who thought that there had been some underhanded work afoot, for my father had not been killed and yet they had killed Mr. Ward. Also they knew that my father came from the State of Pennsylvania and though he never had mentioned it, they knew quite well that he sided with the North. However, Mrs. Ward took up our defense and said that father had warned her husband to leave and go to Siloam Springs. With this bodyguard we reached the Springs without any other misfortune."

After several weeks' imprisonment at Fort Scott, Brother Bishop was set free and through the assistance of General Blunt soon joined his family, at this time staying in Maysville.

With the defeat of the Confederate troops at Fort Wayne, near Beattie's Prairie, on October 22, 1862, by General Blunt's forces, Canaan and Mt. Zion missions were destroyed. Brother Edwin J. Mack was forced to tbandon his post at Canaan, taking his family with him to Missouri. About this time, most of the buildings at New Springplace were destroyed. Many Cherokee members of the Church were killed in the guerilla warfare throughout the nation. Thus, the Moravian Mission that flourished and gave great promise before the War, again was destroyed.

After the capture of Fort Gibson and the defeat of the Confederate forces in Western Arkansas, during the late fall and the winter of 1862-63, Esther Ward and her children lived on an abandoned farm near Maysville, Arkansas, across the line from Beattie's Prairie. She wrote her friends in the North, "To attempt to describe to you all the distress and scenes of trouble that we have witnessed might occupy the pages of a volume, but in the providence of God, we have been preserved."

During the summer of 1863, Brother Mack and his family stayed on the farm near Maysville with Mrs. Ward. Late in the fall, she was again compelled to move her family, this time to Fayetteville, Arkansas, where the Federal troops were stationed. Here she received kind assistance from the Union officers, especially Lieutenant John Dienst and wife, of Sharon, Ohio. A letter to Reverend Gilbert Bishop from Mrs. Ward, dated November 11, 1863, said in part:

"As regards my family, we have had but very little trouble, except from needless fears. We have been hiding our things since you left for fear of being robbed.

"The Indians came to our house, while living near Maysville. They acted rude and savage, had their faces painted and rode their horses through the hall. After sometime, we got them to listen to us, and when we told them that the Crow (Brother Mack's Indian name) was living there, and my father (Dr. Milo Hoyt) and brother (Dr. Hinman Booth Hoyt) were with Col. Phillips Regiment (an Indian Union Regiment), they left. They took, however, Brother Mack's saddle and best shirt.

"The white families on the border of Arkansas fear them very much. The nearest neighbor to Canaan (Brother Mack's Station) named McLaughlin, was cruelly killed in his own house, after taking the oath of allegiance. The two sons of widow Arthur, living also on Beattie's Prairie, were killed and her house burned. The poor woman is almost broken hearted having been robbed of what little was left her. Old grandfather May was killed in his own house; he was over 80 years old and the founder of Maysville. It became a very common thing to to see women dig a grave for sons, husbands or brothers.

"Last summer was a lonely time with us. Brother Mack raised a good garden of vegetables and also some corn. I spent an hour of each day to teach the children of both families. Having my work and family to attend to it was impossible to do more.

"I have also my brother Dr. Hinman Hoyt's little girl, Florence Hoyt, with me. She was left an orphan with none to care for her but myself. I am now here at Fayetteville all alone, with six little children. I feel extremely anxious to get a home where I can take better care of my little charges."

Having expressed the wish to go to West Salem, Illinois, to make her home, Mrs. Ward was advanced sufficient funds for herself and children for the journey from Fayetteville, by Lieutenant Dienst. Having met Brother Mack greatly in need, on her way north, and having given him money, she found herself penniless when she and her children arrived in St. Louis. Friends came to her rescue and supplied her with funds to Olney, Illinois, where she arrived after many hardships on December 23, 1863. Thence, she took the children to West Salem, finding temporary shelter in the home of Reverend Herman Tietze and his wife.

The journal of Reverend Tietze in the Moravian Church records, gives the closing of Esther Ward's story:

"Dec. 28th, 1863: Visited Mrs. Ward, wife of missionary Ward, murdered by the Indians last year. She had arrived here on the Wednesday previous intending to make this her home, with a family of six small children. Find her sick. Mrs. Ward becomes worse.

"Jan. 11th, Monday: Sister Ward fast sinking.

"Tues., Jan. 12, 1864, Sister Ward breathed her last at 1 3/4 P. M. Her oldest son, a lad of 9 years, is to live with me for the present.

"Wed. 13th: Funeral of Sister Ward. Rev. Houser kept it."

THE WARD CHILDREN

With her arrival in West Salem, the whole aim and purpose of Esther Ward's life, since the death of her husband, had been accomplished: She had brought the six small children in her care to safety. Of these, her own were Darius, Lydia, Clara, and the twins, William and Henry. There was also Florence Hoyt, her five year old niece.

Through the efforts of Brother Tietze, temporary homes were found for all the children. According to its ruling at that time, the Moravian Church provided five years' schooling in one of three schools for girls, and one school for boys, as part of the missionary's annual salary or fifty dollars a year. Under this system, the children were maintained, fed, and clothed, each widely separated from his brothers and sisters. Many years later when they were grown, they were reunited with their relatives and friends in the Cherokee Nation.

DARIUS E. WARD

Darius E. Ward was born at Beattie's Prairie, on November 23, 1854, the eldest son of James and Esther (Hoyt) Ward. Darius' Cherokee name was *Kee-too-wha-gi*. The tragedy of his father's death having made an indelible impression upon him, his one ambition as a lad was to meet up with the man who had assassinated his father.

After the death of his mother from pneumonia, the lad remained in the homes of Reverend Tietz and of Reverend Hayman for a short time, in West Salem, Illinois. For five years, he attended Nazareth Hall, the Moravian school for boys, at Nazareth, Pennsylvania, also attended by several Cherokee boys of the Ross family. After completing his studies here, Darius was apprenticed four and a half years to William Wolp & Co., cabinetmakers, of Bethlehem, Pennsylvania. For a time, he also received instruction in house building in Philadelphia.

On November 20, 1875, he married Sarah Caroline Ritter, at Bethlehem. Ten children were born of this marriage. In 1876, Mr. and Mrs. Ward made their home at Vinita, Indian

Territory, where he was a builder and contractor, doing a large business throughout the country. In 1884, he moved to Tahlequah, where he soon took charge of J. W. Stapler's hardware establishment. In 1887, Mr. Ward was appointed building inspector in the Cherokee Nation, during his term serving as inspector of the new Female Seminary building at Tahlequah. Mrs. Ward died on February 29, 1896. On August 9, 1897, Mr. Ward married Mrs. Mary Murphy (ne'e Hester) and two children were born of this marriage.

In the prime of life, Darius E. Ward was described as a man of good, common sense, "courteous in manner and address." In appearance, he was five feet ten inches in height and his average weight was about 180 pounds.

Throughout his active life, he was a staunch member and lay worker in the Moravian Church. He was a member of Knights of Pythias, secretary of the Cherokee "Old Settlers Commissioners," and in 1900, elected member of the Cherokee Board of Education. After Oklahoma became a State, he was elected county commissioner of Cherokee County, 1910. He died at Collinsville, Tulsa County, on June 22, 1930.

Lydia Ann Ward

Lydia Ann Ward was born on August 1, 1856, the daughter of James and Esther (Hoyt) Ward. After the loss of her parents, she was cared for in the home of Reverend Herman Tieze's family in West Salem, Illinois, until she was ten years old. She grew up a beautiful girl and was educated at the Moravian Seminary, Bethlehem, Pennsylvania. On September 10, 1875, she was married to William Clifford Chamberlain. They later made their home at Vinita, Indian Territory, and were the parents of three daughters, Edith, Flora, and Clara. Edith died as an infant. Florence died of phthisis at the age of eighteen, just before she was to have graduated from high school at Vinita. Mrs. Chamberlain

DARIUS E. WARD

died at the age of twenty-six, on July 26, 1882. Her surviving daughter, Clara, later married H. Alvis Cardwell, of Maypearl, Texas.

HENRY JULIUS AND WILLIAM WEST WARD

Henry Julius and William West Ward were born on May 12, 1862, at New Springplace, Cherokee Nation. They were the twin sons and youngest children of James and Esther (Hoyt) Ward. Only a little over a year old when they had lost both parents, they were cared for under the direction of the Moravian Church and educated at Nazareth Hall, Bethlehem, Pennsylvania. Henry married Emma Luchenbach, and William, Roxanna Sterner, both of Bethlehem. Henry Julius Ward died on November 24, 1933, at Enid, Oklahoma, and was buried in the Enid cemetery. William W. and Roxanna (Sterner) Ward were the parents of one son, Herman Henry Ward.

CLARA A. WARD AND NEW SPRINGPLACE TO-DAY

On Sunday, July 2, 1939, Miss Clara Alice Ward visited the site of New Springplace Mission, the place of her birth. She was baptised as a three weeks old infant on Sunday, October 9, 1859, in the church of this early day Moravian Mission, by Reverend Gilbert Bishop.

On her memorable visit to New Springplace last July, Miss Ward was accompanied by Darius E. Ward's eldest son, J. Herbert Ward, his wife, and their eldest son, George Herbert Ward; and by Doratha Ludema (Ward) Poole, granddaughter of Darius E. Ward, and eldest daughter of his fourth child, James D. Ward.

Driving to the west edge of the village of Oaks, in Delaware County, they continued on several hundred yards, finally following a footpath to the ruined rock wall still surrounding the old spring. Here they drank from the sparkling cold water. Near at hand was the clear mountain stream called Spring Creek. The New Springplace church building had disappeared long ago, nothing remaining except a stone doorstep in a clump of buck-berry bushes to mark the site.

Several months before the Cherokee Treaty of 1866 had been signed with the United States, re-establishing the rights of the Cherokees after the War, Unity's Mission Board of the Moravian Church at Herrnhüt forwarded word to Salem, N. C., to recommence the work in the Cherokee Nation. Thus, the Moravian Mission was the first of the old missions begun in the nation after the War. In July, 1866, Reverend Edwin J. Mack returned to New Springplace where he found some of the old buildings standing though in a dilapidated condition. Everywhere the country was a scene of desolation; former homes were in ashes and farms laid waste.

On June 1, 1867, Reverend Mack preached the funeral sermon of Chief John Ross by special invitation of the Cherokee National Council, a signal honor for the Moravian Church. At the earnest request of Mrs. Jane Ross Nave, daughter of Chief Ross, Brother Mack began holding regular church services at Tahlequah. Mrs. Nave had attended the Moravian Female Academy at Salem, in 1835-37. During the War, she and her children lived in Bethlehem, Pennsylvania. Here, in February, 1867, she was received as a member of the Moravian Church, where 125 years before Count Zinzendorf had baptised one of the first Indian converts.

In traveling through the Cherokee Nation after the War, Brother Mack was heartily welcomed by old time friends and a number of Moravian Church members among the full-blood Cherokees. Before many years had passed the mission work was growing steadily, new missionaries having been sent into this field by the directors in Salem. In 1892, church services were well attended and membership increasing at several places, of which the principal stations were Woodmount, two miles south of Tahlequah; New Springplace; Ulm Chapel, three miles west of Springplace; Washburne's

CLARA ALICE WARD.
at 13 years.

Mill School, ten miles west of Springplace; Braggs, present Muskogee County; Mohr's, four miles east of Braggs; and White Oak, sixteen miles south of Tahlequah.

During this promising period, the "Missionary Wards" still carried on. Darius E. Ward and his wife were active and dependable members in the Sunday school and as lay workers in their home communities and at New Springplace and at Woodmount.

The Moravian Church continued its work until the passage of the Curtis Act by Congress, in 1898, which provided the first steps leading to the close of the Cherokee government. The village of Oaks having been established about a half mile from New Springplace, Reverend N. L. Nielson, a Lutheran missionary from Denmark, opened a mission school in the village, in 1902, mostly attended by Cherokees. In the fall of that year, he organized a church with about twenty Moravian Church members. This new mission and church grew to over 200 members in twenty years and marks the village of Oaks to-day. Reverend Nielson had been associated with the Moravians in the Cherokee Nation from 1892 and rejoiced in carrying on the work, saying that it was as if he had found his "own people and church."

Some years ago, Miss Ward began gathering incidents of the life story of her father and mother and their families. Leaving the spring on their visit in 1939, to the site of the mission, the members of her party walked through a field to the old Springplace cemetery. Here the simple inscription on a marble slab gave fresh inspiration to memorialize the life of her parents:

Sept. 2nd, 1862

JAMES WARD

A

MISSIONARY

GENEALOGY OF THE LOWRY FAMILY OF THE CHEROKEE NATION

Oo-lu-tsa (She's come) a fullblood Cherokee woman was the mother of:

Che-kaw-nah-ler (Forget me not) and Nancy.

GENERATION NUMBER 1

George Lowry, a Scotchman, married Nancy.

THEIR CHILDREN:

#2 Capt. John Lowry	Married	Betsy Shorey
#2 Major George Lowry	"	Lucy Benge
#2 Jane Lowry	"	Taluntiski
#2 Sallie Lowry	"	Staydt (Rope)
#2 Betsy Lowry	"	John Sevier
#2 Nelly Lowry	"	Edmond Fallen
#2 Akey Lowry	"	———— Burnes

GENERATION NUMBER 2

#2 Major George Lowry married Lucy Benge.

THEIR CHILDREN:

#3 James Lowry	Married	Betsy McLemore
#3 George Lowry	"	Betsy Baldridge
#3 Susan Lowry	"	Andrew Ross
#3 Lydia Lowry	"	Milo Hoyt
#3 Rachel Lowry	"	(1st) David Brown
	"	(2nd) Nelson Orr
#3 John Lowry (Died in youth)		
#3 Anderson Lowry	"	Mary Nave
#3 Arch Lowry	"	Delia Baldridge
#3 Washington Lowry	"	Nancy Guest, daughter of Sequoyah

GENERATION NUMBER 3

#3 Lydia Lowry married Dr. Milo Hoyt, son of Rev. Ard Hoyt.

THEIR CHILDREN:

#4 Dolly Eunice Hoyt	Married	Rev. Nelson Chamberlain
#4 Anna Hoyt	"	Rev. Hamilton Balentine
#4 Hinman Booth Hoyt	"	(1st) Ruth Buffington
	"	(2nd) Elizabeth Candy
#4 Sarah Hoyt	"	Richard Hunter
#4 Lucy L. Hoyt	"	Monroe Keys
#4 Esther Hoyt	"	Rev. James Ward
#4 Milo Ard Hoyt	"	Harriet Fulsom Washburn
#4 George Hoyt (Supposed to have died in Kansas.)		

GENERATION NUMBER 4

#4 Esther Hoyt married Rev. James Ward.

THEIR CHILDREN:

#5 Darius E. Ward ....Married (1st) Sarah Ritter
                                    "   (2nd) Mary (Hester)
                                              Murphy
#5 Lydia Ann Ward ....   "   William C. Chamberlain
#5 Clara Alice Ward (Professional Nurse, R. N., Bellevue Hospital of
        New York, N. Y.)
#5 William W. Ward ....Married Roxanna Sterner
#5 Henry J. Ward ....   "   Emma Luckenbach

GENERATION NUMBER 5

#5 Darius E. Ward married (1st) Sarah C. Ritter.

THEIR CHILDREN:

#6 Minnie E. Ward ....Married Boone Gray
#6 J. Herbert Ward ....   "   Hettie Fowler
#6 James D. Ward ....Married (1st) Grace Hill
                                             (2nd) Sadie Turk
#6 Leslie O. Ward ....(Died aged 4 years.)
#6 Clara E. Ward ....(Died aged 7 months.)
#6 Hinman H. Ward ....(Died aged 20½ years.)
#6 Sydney R. Ward ....(Died aged 24 years.)
#6 Gertrude I. Ward........................Married Claud Johnson
#6 R. Lee Ward ....(Died in infancy.)
#6 Ruth E. Ward ....Married Harry Ghan
#6 Sarah Ruby Ward ....   "   Omer Brown

#5 Darius E. Ward married (2nd) Mary (Hester) Murphy.

THEIR CHILDREN:

#6 Martha A. Ward........................Married John Hartness
#6 Rebecca L. Ward ....(Died aged 2 years)

#5 Lydia Ann Ward married William Chamberlain.

THEIR CHILDREN:

#6 Edith Chamberlain ....(Died in infancy)
#6 Flora Chamberlain ....(Died. Age unknown.)
#6 Clara Chamberlain ....Married H. Alvis Cardwell

---

#5 Clara Alice Ward—Single.

#5 William W. Ward married Roxanna Sterner.

THEIR CHILDREN:

#6 Herman Henry Ward

#5 Henry J. Ward married Emma Luckenbach.

GENERATION NUMBER 6

#6 Minnie E. Ward married Boone Gray.

THEIR CHILDREN:

#7 Barto Gray ....(Born April 17, 1898)
#7 Sonora Irene Gray ....(Born August 4, 1906)
#7 Clara Lucille Gray ....(Born May 9, 1903)

WILLIAM W. and HENRY J. WARD,
Twin Brothers.

#6 J. Herbert Ward married Hettie Fowler.
THEIR CHILDREN:

#7 George Herbert Ward ....(Born Oct. 14, 1904)
#7 Clara Dott Ward ....(Born Sept. 28, 1906)
#7 Blanche J. Ward ....(Born March 6, 1908)
#7 Esther V. Ward ....(Born April 11, 1911)
#7 Violet Margaretta Ward ....(Born March 2, 1913)

#6 James D. Ward married (1st) Oma Grace Hill.
THEIR CHILDREN:

#7 Doratha Ludema Ward ....(Born Feb. 14, 1906)
#7 Florence Oma Grace Ward ......(Born Oct. 23, 1908)

#6 James D. Ward married (2nd) Sadie Turk.
THEIR CHILDREN:

#7 James Cornelius Ward ....(Born July 9, 1912)
#7 Bernard Owen Ward ....(Born Oct. 16, 1913)

#6 Gertrude Irene Ward married Claud Johnson.
THEIR CHILDREN:

#7 Ruth Illa Johnson ....(Born August 29, 1908.)
#7 Ross Mayes Johnson ....(Died age 3½ years.)
#7 Nina Marie Johnson ....(Born Oct. 14, 1913.)

#6 Ruth Edna Ward married Harry Ghan.
THEIR CHILDREN:

#7 Harold F. Ghan ....(Born June 20, 1911.)
#7 James H. Ghan ....(Born July 23, 1913.)

#6 Sarah Ruby Ward married Omar Brown.
THEIR CHILD:

#7 Ruby Catherine Brown ....(Born Oct. 9, 1914.)

#6 Martha A. Ward married John Hartness.

GENERATION NUMBER 4 (Continued)

#4 Dolly Eunice Hoyt married Rev. Nelson Chamberlain.

THEIR CHILDREN:

#5 Beacher Chamberlain
#5 William Chamberlain
#5 Edward Chamberlain
#5 Abbie Chamberlain
#5 Arthur Chamberlain
#5 Robert Chamberlain

———

#4 Lucy L. Hoyt married Monroe Keys.

THEIR CHILDREN:

#5 Mary Eunice Keys	Married	Hamilton Balentine, Jr.
#5 Lydia Emma Keys	"	Charles J. Taylor
#5 Fannie Keys	"	James A. Leforce
#5 Sarah Ann Keys	"	Samuel J. Leforce
#5 Lizzie Keys	"	Oren S. Athey
#5 Monroe A. Keys	"	
#5 Lucy Keys	"	John Miles

———

#4 Anna Hoyt married Rev. Hamilton Balentine.

THEIR CHILDREN:

#5 William Balentine	Married	(1st) Fannie Keys (2nd) _____ Johnson
#5 Hamilton Balentine	"	Mary E. Keys
#5 Jonathon Balentine	"	Lizzie Foreman

———

#4 Hinman Booth Hoyt married (1st) Ruth Ann Buffington; (2nd) Elizabeth Candy.

The Child of Hinman Booth and Ruth Buffington Hoyt:
#5 Florence Ellen Hoyt.

GENERATION NUMBER 5

#5 Florence Ellen Hoyt married (1st) Joel Cowan McSpadden (son of Rev. T. K. B. and Elizabeth Green McSpadden); (2nd) A. L. Lyons.

The Children of Florence Hoyt and Joel Cowan McSpadden:

#6 Thomas Booth McSpadden
#6 Ella Bailey McSpadden
#6 Elizabeth Peach McSpadden
#6 Maude Hoyt McSpadden
#6 Forrest Kavanaugh McSpadden (Died Oct. 12, 1904)
#6 Theodore Raymond McSpadden
#6 Oscar Lyle McSpadden (Died Sept., 1939)

MRS. A. L. LYONS
Formerly, Mrs. Joel C. (Florence Hoyt) McSpadden

GENERATION NUMBER 6

#6 Thomas Booth McSpadden married (1st) Rhoda Caulk (Died).
THEIR CHILD:
#7 Harriet Haskell McSpadden

#6 Thomas Booth McSpadden married (2nd) Ona Baines.
THEIR CHILDREN:
#7 Opal McSpadden
#7 Harold Booth McSpadden
#7 Louise McSpadden
#7 Lyle Jesse McSpadden
#7 Katherine McSpadden
#7 Robert McSpadden
#7 Billie McSpadden
#7 Jack McSpadden

#6 Ella Bailey McSpadden married Harry L. Morrison.

#6 Elizabeth Peach McSpadden married J. Bartly Milam.
THEIR CHILDREN:
#7 Hinman Stuart Milam
#7 Mildred E. Milam
#7 Mary E. Milam

#6 Maude Hoyt McSpadden married Woodley Gail Phillips.
THEIR CHILDREN:
#7 Joel Arthur Phillips (Died Dec. 13, 1914)
#7 Donald Mortimer Phillips
#7 Ross Marvin Phillips
#7 Laurence Gail Phillips
#7 Paul McSpadden Phillips
#7 John Woodley Phillips

#6 Theodore Raymond McSpadden married Buelah Thomason.
THEIR CHILDREN:
#7 Elizabeth McSpadden ....Married Kenneth Lieb
#7 Ruth Ann McSpadden
#7 Mary Nell McSpadden

#6 Oscar Lyle McSpadden married (1st) Georgia Craig.
THEIR CHILD:
#7 Craig McSpadden

#6 Oscar Lyle McSpadden married (2nd) Irene Sloan.
THEIR CHILD:
#7 Florence Ellen McSpadden

GENERATION NUMBER 7

#7 Harriet Haskell McSpadden married Robert Buttermore.
THEIR CHILD:
#8 Rhoma Clair Buttermore

#7 Opal McSpadden married Odell Hampton.

#7 Harold Booth (Cap) McSpadden married Louise Draeger.
THEIR CHILD:
#8 Larry Earl McSpadden

#7 Hinman Stuart Milam married Katherine Burris.
THEIR CHILDREN:
#8 Dian Milam
#8 William Gynn Milam

#7 Mildred E. Milam married Phillip Viles.
THEIR CHILD:
#8 Jonas Viles II

#7 Mary E. Milam married George Joseph Stevenson.
THEIR CHILD:
#8 George Joseph Stevenson III

#7 Donald Mortimer Phillips married (1st) Bettie Ostrander.
THEIR CHILD:
#8 Donna Mae Phillips
#7 Donald Mortimer Phillips married (2nd) Revelle Davis.
THEIR CHILD:
#8 Donald Michael Phillips

#7 Ross Marvin Phillips married Laura Baker.
THEIR CHILD:
#8 Barbara McSpadden Phillips

GENEALOGY OF THE WARD FAMILY OF THE CHEROKEE NATION

"Granny" Hopper, a fullblood Cherokee woman, married ....
McDaniel, a Scotchman
THEIR CHILDREN:
Alexander McDaniel
Lewis McDaniel
Catherine ("Katie") McDaniel

GENERATION NUMBER 1

#1 John (Jack) Ward from Ireland married Catherine McDaniel.
THEIR CHILDREN:
#2 James Ward
#2 George Ward
#2 Samuel Ward
#2 Charles Ward
#2 Bryant Ward
#2 Betsy Ward
#2 Susie Ward
#2 Nancy Lucy Ward

GENERATION NUMBER 2

#2 James Ward, Sr., married (1st) Sarah Redding (Died):
(2nd) Lucy Hainy.

THE CHILDREN OF JAMES AND LUCY HAINY WARD:

#3 Catherine Ward ....Married Joseph Keeton
#3 John (Jack) Ward ....(Died. No issue)
#3 Thomas Ward ....Married Mary Hicks
#3 Moses Ward .... " ....Lear
#3 Bryant Ward .... " Martha Kinchlo
#3 George Ward .... " .... Kinchlo
#3 James Ward, Jr. .... " Esther Hoyt
#3 Lucy Ward .... " James Williams
#3 Roxanna Ward .... " Dan Tittle
#3 Nancy Ward .... " Cal Dean Gunter

GENERATION NUMBER 3

#3 James Ward, jr., married Esther Hoyt.

THEIR CHILDREN:

#4 Darius E. Ward
#4 Lydia Ann Ward
#4 Clara Alice Ward
#4 William W. Ward } Twins
#4 Henry J. Ward

FOR MARRIAGES AND DESCENDANTS SEE LOWRY FAMILY HISTORY

#3 Catherine Ward married Joseph Keeton.

THEIR CHILDREN:

#4 Lucy Keeton ....Married ....Dial
#4 Nancy Keeton .... " ....Dial
#4 Patsy Keeton .... " ....Martin

#3 Jack Ward—Died without issue.

#3 Thomas Ward married Mary Hicks.

THEIR CHILDREN:

#4 Rosanna Ward ....Married ....Martin
#4 John T. Ward ....
#4 Julia A. Ward .... " ....Thompson
#4 Barbara Ward .... " ....Steward
#4 James Ward ....
#4 George Oscar Ward ....
#4 Thomas C. Ward ....
#4 Sarah C. Ward .... " ....Robertson
#4 Lucy Ward .... " ....Shelly
#4 Ellen Ward .... " ....Bradshaw
#4 Daniel M. Ward ....

#3 Moses Ward married.....................................Lear.

THEIR CHILDREN:

#4 Thomas Ward ....
#4 James M. Ward ....
#4 Cal Dean Ward ....
#4 Joel Ward ....
#4 Josephine Ward ....Married Charlie Franks
#4 Helen Ward ....   "   Rod Perry

---

#3 Bryant Ward married Martha Kinchlo.

THEIR CHILDREN:

#4 Elizabeth Ward ....Married ....Swim
#4 Emaline Ward ....   "   ....Bean
#4 Nancy Ward ....   "   ....Francis
#4 Esther Ward ....
#4 John Ward ....
#4 James Ward ....
#4 Jasper Ward ....
#4 Cornelius Ward ....

#3 George Ward married (1st) ....Kinchlo.

THEIR CHILDREN:

#4 Elizabeth Ward ....Married ....Kelly
#4 Lucy Ward ....
#4 Alexander Ward ....

#3 George Ward married (2nd) ....Townsend.

THEIR CHILDREN:

#4 Francis Ward ....Married R. Hosey
#4 Martha Ward ....   "   Bud Thomas
#4 Carrie Ward ....
#4 John Ward ....
#4 Gel Ward ....
#4 James Ward ....

#3 Lucy Ward married James Williams.

THEIR CHILDREN:

#4 Martha Williams ....Married ....Thompson
#4 Nancy Williams ....   "   George Eaton

#3 Rosanna Ward married Dan Tittle.

THEIR CHILDREN:

#4 Permelia Tittle ....Married A. Sager
#4 James Tittle ....
#4 Robert Tittle ....
#4 Dora Tittle ....   "   Robert Dobkins
#4 Ellen Tittle ....   "   Jake Heiser
#4 Susie Tittle ....   "   Doctor Wimer

#3 Nancy Ward married Cal Dan Gunter.

THEIR CHILDREN:

#4 Ann Elizabeth Gunter	Married	G. Chandler
#4 Lucy Gunter	"	Doctor Fortner
#4 Olevia Gunter	"	............Marrs
#4 Lovina Gunter	"	L. Duckworth
#4 John Gunter		
#4 Nancy Gunter	"	............Alfrey
#4 Amy Gunter	"	............Alfrey
#4 Cal Dean		

The foregoing is the direct lineage of the **Ward Family,** no further removed than first cousins.

INDEX

Made in the USA
Monee, IL
04 March 2023

29140559R00059